Making Peace With My Mother

by

Sylvia B. Grossman

Knowledge, Ideas & Trends
KIT
Publisher
Manchester, CT 06040

Cover Art: Gil Fahey
Text Design: Cindy Parker

First Published in 1992 by:
        Knowledge, Ideas & Trends, Inc.
        1131-0 Tolland Turnpike, Suite 175
        Manchester, CT 06040

Library of Congress Cataloging-in-Publication Data

CIP: 92-12917
ISBN: 1-879198-07-X

1. Mothers and Daughters - United States - Case Studies.
2. Grossman, Sylvia, B. 3. Daughters - United States -
Biography.

10 9 8 7 6 5 4 3 2 1

First Edition
Printed in the United States of America

To my dear husband Bernard, who helped me so much

> with this book,
> with my mother,
> with my life,

And to Amos who helped change its course.

Acknowledgements

I am greatly indebted to my friends, Alice Lippman, Cathy
Frank and Sunnie Meyer, who read every word of this book
and all from whom I have drawn ideas and inspiration; to Bart
Midwood of the New York Studio for Writers, for his encouragement and support when *Making Peace With My Mother*
was just the germ of an idea; and to my editor, Rita
McCullough, for her skillful and sensitive guidance and editing.

Table of Contents

Part 1

A Summons to the Past

Chapter One

I was in my kitchen cooking my specialty, duck with cherry sauce, for the surprise birthday dinner I was making for my husband when the phone rang. As I turned to wipe my hands, my glance was caught by my favorite birch heaped with fleecy snow. Beyond it, a mist glowed over Long Island Sound. I smiled. The phone rang again.

"Yes?"

"Mrs. Grossman?"

"Yes."

"You're Mrs. Berman's daughter?"

I caught my breath. "How did you find me?"

"Took all day."

"Who is this?"

"Mr. Amman. I'm the Super in your mother's building." He spoke with an accent of indecipherable origin.

"Mrs. Grossman, your mother nearly got killed this morning. She all but fell into the incinerator."

"What? What are you saying? How did that happen?"

"Mrs. Grossman, your mother is how old?"

"I don't know. Eighty-two. Eighty-four." She had always been cagey about her age.

"And she's all of four foot eight. We have a very big incinerator. She was bending over to put something in."

"Oh, my god!"

"Also, she's practically blind."

"What are you talking about? Since when?"

"Since a few weeks. But you wouldn't know. You never see her."

His disapproval of me seeped through the telephone wires.

I plunked down in a chair, overwhelmed with guilt. It was

true. Except for the one day of my father's funeral, three months ago, I had hardly seen my mother in twenty years.

"Mr. Amman, I'll call her immediately. And I'll be over first thing in the morning. Thank you very much for your concern and for calling me."

But he had hung up.

I called my mother immediately. The line was busy. How could her line be busy, I wondered. My mother had no friends. She was not on speaking terms with any relatives. My brother Mitch, whom she adored, called her from Los Angeles for ten minutes twice a year. How could her line be busy? There was only one possibility. She had unknowingly placed something under the receiver, and it was off the hook.

I took the following day off from work, made the long trip to Brighton Beach, and rang my mother's bell at 9 A.M. No answer. I had no way of entering her apartment building unless she buzzed. I rang again. Still no answer. I waited ten minutes till someone else walked into the building and followed them through the door. I took the elevator to the sixth floor and rang my mother's doorbell. Again no answer. I banged on the door. I knew better than to have the super let me in with his key. My mother would consider that an invasion of her privacy and be furious.

On the fifth ring, my mother, finally, opened the door a crack. Her face was closed as a fist.

"Oh, it's you." She slammed the door in my face.

My old anger at my mother, which I had been trying to control for decades, rose up in me.

I kept pressing the bell. Eventually, she answered the door a second time.

I forced my way in, brushing past her. The phone was indeed off the hook. I put it back in its cradle. I looked around the living room. A thick layer of dust lay over everything. In the kitchen, the baseboards were lined with broken crockery, dried orange peels, bread crusts. This was so unlike my mother!

"Ma, what's happening with you?"

"Oh, finally, you're interested?"

"Ma. I'm here. I'm here to help you. I see you're having trouble seeing. You're holding on to the wall."

"Oh, that's nothing. Since Pa died, I can't see. It was the shock."

"Ma, it was not the shock. It could be galloping glaucoma or God knows what else. You have to see an eye doctor, immediately."

"You're not going to think for me. What makes you so smart?"

I steeled myself. I knew if I allowed my anger to take over, I wouldn't be able to think straight or cope with her at all.

"Ma, in my entire life, you never gave me credit for having any brains. I know what I'm talking about."

"I don't need you of all people to make decisions for me."

"Ma, for heaven's sake! It's urgent! How long is it since you've begun to have trouble with your eyes?"

"I told you. Since Pa died. A little later. It was the shock. I don't need a doctor."

I began to call ophthalmologists. Finally, I found one able to give us an appointment that afternoon.

"Ma, listen. I'll take you out to a nice lunch in Sheepshead Bay. Then, we have an appointment with the eye doctor at 1:30."

"I'm not going."

"Why not? Maybe it's something we can still catch in time. Every minute may count."

"I'm not letting you, of all people, take me by the hand and drag me to a doctor like a child. I can still take care of myself."

"Ma, please. This is no time to be stubborn."

"Zviah, who gave you the right to tell me what to do? The nerve! The chutspah!"

Despite everything I had learned in therapy, I began to seethe.

"Ma, you're enough to -" I stopped myself. "Ma, you want me to just forget about you and leave you here all alone when you can't see? Is that what you want? The floor is full of broken dishes. The super says you nearly fell into the incinerator."

My mother sat herself down in the rocking chair, gripped the wooden armrests so hard her knuckles showed white, pursed her lips, and refused to budge or say another word. I had to cancel the appointment.

I rang the bell of her next door neighbor, a thin, grey-haired woman, named Ann Rabinowitz.

I explained my predicament and asked her if she'd be kind enough to please look in on my mother once in a while till I found someone to stay with her. She said she would.

"I may know someone for you if you're interested," she added.

"You do?" I wanted to kiss her.

"Well, Aliza Katz is a very kind woman who's been unfortunate and had a pretty hard life. She's a Holocaust survivor and - well, we won't go into that. The point is, she's much more highly educated than most people you'll get and comes very well recommended. She took care of my niece's mother-in-law. They can't sing her praises enough."

"She sounds wonderful. Ann, you're saving my life."

I called Mrs. Katz immediately and interviewed her in her Queens apartment. She was small and soft and rounded, with sad eyes but a warm smile. I sensed she was a kind, gentle person, liked her immediately, and had her start work that afternoon.

* * *

I was very busy with my guests that evening and attended a conference over the weekend.

Very early Monday morning, before I left for work, I received a phone call from my mother.

"Just a minute," I said. "Let me get a robe. It's cold in the house."

"What do you mean, it's cold? Your husband can't see to it that you have a warm house?"

"Ma, oil is expensive. Let me just get into a robe."

"Why should you save money for him? I bet you don't even know how much money he has!"

I said quietly. "Ma, you say one more word against Bernie and you'll never hear from me again." I waited for that to sink in. "Now what's the problem?"

"I called to tell you about the kind of woman you picked out for me. You really know how to pick them. From out of the gutter!"

I sighed in exasperation. "Let me talk to Mrs. Katz."

Mrs. Katz came to the phone. She seemed to be in tears.

"I was going to call you a little later at work, Mrs. Grossman."

"What happened, Mrs. Katz?"

"Mrs. Grossman, I don't know how to say this. I feel so terrible I can't help you out. But I simply can't stay with your mother."

"What happened?"

"Mrs. Grossman, don't ask."

"What, Mrs. Katz?"

"Nothing. I like you. I don't want to upset you."

"I want to know."

"Mrs. Grossman, let me put it this way. I spent two years in a concentration camp. And I just spent two days with your mother. Believe me. These two days were worse."

"Oh Lord! What in the world will I do with her now? Look, Mrs. Katz, maybe it's just a question of getting to understand each other. I'll pay you an extra twenty dollars a week."

"Could you pick me up some time today?"

"Mrs. Katz, please. Won't you try to stay at least for another day or two till I find someone else? Please! I can't leave her alone!"

"Mrs. Grossman, I have my health to consider. You mother is, how shall I put it without hurting your feelings, a mean, angry bitter woman. I don't envy you."

* * *

That night after work, Bernie and I arrived at my mother's home It looked a lot neater. Mrs. Katz was packed and ready to go. I motioned her to wait.

"How are you, Ma?" I kissed her.

She glared at me. "I see you brought him."

"Hello, Dvorah," Bernie kissed her, too. "Yes, Zvi brought me. And I brought her."

The joke was lost on my mother.

"One thing I've never understood, Bernie. What do you see in her?"

Bernie caught my eye and raised his brows.

"I don't think you should talk about your daughter that way," he said in his mild way.

"She's a terrible housekeeper, isn't she? It's not my fault. I tried to teach her how to do things in the house. She'd never listen to me. Absolutely impossible. How do you put up with her?"

I gritted my teeth.

"Ma," I said, "I know you don't want to go to the ophthalmologist with me. But Bernie has offered to take a day off from work and drive you. Isn't that nice of him? Will you go with him?"

"I once saw an eye doctor while Pa was alive. Even before his last stroke. He said there was nothing he could do."

"Which doctor?"

"I can't remember."

"What did he mean there's nothing he can do? What did he say was wrong?"

"None of your business."

Bernie moved closer to me and spoke out of the corner of his mouth.

"Zvi, we're wasting our time. Let's get out of here."

"What did he say? You're talking behind my back?"

*　*　*

Bernie and I drove Mrs. Katz back to Queens.

Then we treated ourselves to a lavish dinner. We felt we deserved it after what we had been through. But we both just toyed with our food.

All that evening with my mother, I had kept a tight rein on my anxieties. Now, suddenly, they broke through and rushed at me. I stabbed a tomato wedge with my fork as if I hated it.

"Bernie, this whole thing's tearing me apart. She's worse than ever. You have no idea what an effort, all those years of therapy, it took for me to detach myself from her so nothing she said could rile me. And now, it's as if everything... as if everything I struggled so hard for..." I burst into tears. "Bernie, she's going to wreck our marriage."

Bernie took my icy hands in his and rubbed them. "Aw, come on, darling. Have a little faith in me. She won't wreck our marriage."

"She's always gnawing at it. I'm afraid she'll wear us down. Bernie, we must keep away from her. Yet there's no way I can. She's almost blind. If I leave her alone, she's sure to fall into the incinerator or have some other horrible accident. Then, I become a murderess. She can't stay alone. But no one will stay with her." My hands began to flutter.

"The solution is to put her into a Home for the Aged Blind."

"Are you kidding? You know what she's like. She'll refuse to go. Besides, all these places pick and choose their people. They would never accept someone like her."

"Zvi, you're driving yourself up a wall. There must be some solution. We just have to find it."

"Yeah? Okay. Give me a solution. Go ahead."

Bernie couldn't look at me.

"You have one?"

"Well, I - I" He kept a straight face. "We could shoot her."

I could not even muster a smile.

"I mean it. What are we going to do with her? You're not going to suggest we take her home with us?"

A look of horror crossed his face.

"You see?"

He sighed. "I don't know - I just -" He stared helplessly at his lobster and pushed away his almost untouched plate. "In addition to everything else, the way she treats you makes me nauseous."

I was so touched. Anything I could say seemed inadequate. I squeezed his hand. My eyes brimmed.

He stroked the nape of my neck.

I closed my eyes and sighed. "Oh, that's good, darling." I leaned up against him.

He held my head against his shoulder, smoothing my hair. "You know, dear, you've never talked about your mother's life. How in the world did she ever get that way?"

Chapter 2

"There's so much to tell about my mother," I started later that night. Bernie and I were lying on warm pillows with the light from the open fire flickering on our faces. "And some of it is so ugly. You got a whiff of it tonight. I really wanted to spare you, darling. And the whole subject is so painful to me."

"I don't want to probe if it's going to hurt you so much."

I heaved a deep sigh. "No. It looks as if we're going to be exposed to her from now on so I suppose it's time that you know what there is to know." My eyes filled. "Bernie, from the day I was born, she never said a good word to me."

He patted my hand. "It began so early."

"When I was a child, I pushed everything about my relationship with her out of my mind so I would just be able to live."

I stopped again, reliving the pain.

"I talked about it a lot in therapy with Amos, of course. But, after I worked most of it out, I folded the memories neatly back into their box again until I saw her tonight."

I put my head on his shoulder. We watched the small flames along the glowing log.

"Hearing the things she said tonight reawakened so much. Okay. Let's see. What do I know about how mother got that way?"

"Did she ever reveal anything to you about her life before she met your father?"

"You might think that, having the relationship we did, she wouldn't have talked to me about herself. The strange thing is that she did. For her own reasons, of course. Not to build a bond between us. Or to share things with me as her daughter. But because she had no one else to talk to, and she desperately needed to remember what a beautiful girl she had been and how much better she could have done than to marry my father. Also, how superior she was to me. At least, that's what Amos thought."

"Go on."

"She never tired of telling me that everyone said that she, the eldest, was the most beautiful of all the seven Koppel sisters. She had shining black hair, deep black eyes, and a perfect olive complexion. She was petite, dainty, graceful, with tiny feet of which she was inordinately proud. She had a rich singing voice, a mezzo soprano. In her twenties, she was actually accepted in the Odessa Synagogue Choir, the finest Jewish Choir in all of Europe. No mean honor. She was dying to train to sing Opera."

"She studied Opera?"

"No. Her father wouldn't hear of it. Girls of her class didn't exhibit themselves in public. One more thing. She knew how to sew and could dress elegantly on little money."

"Okay. So Dvorah is beautiful and can sing."

"Also, according to her sisters whom I met in Israel, she was a very happy young girl."

Bernie's mouth relaxed in a slow smile. "Your mother happy? She looks as tight lipped and suspicious as if she's afraid someone might be enjoying themselves somewhere!"

"That's it! She must have changed drastically somewhere along the way."

He shook his head. "Sounds incredible!"

"Bernie, I think I really began in the wrong place. Dvorah's whole story makes no sense unless you see it in the context of her family. You see, her father, my grandfather, was this great Talmudic scholar with a majestic forked beard, who came from a long dynasty of *gaonim*."

"Gaonim?"

"Talmudic geniuses. He allowed himself the privilege of having thirteen children but never managed to earn a living for them so, naturally, he had no dowries for his seven daughters. My mother has told me with great pride that for decades her father used to pronounce once a week, 'The Koppel *yichus*, you know, lineage, is a dowry in itself.'"

Bernie chuckled. "Got him off the hook."

"Well, to some extent it was true. The prestige of the family in Odessa was such that many young men sought his daughters in marriage. My grandfather considered himself a liberal and wouldn't stoop to matchmakers. The preferred method was for a suitor to present himself on Saturday afternoons and drink endless cups of tea from the samovar while Noah and his eldest son, the Crown Prince, Dovid, the one who later became an important writer in Israel, could scrutinize him and pass judgment. Sometimes four or five suitors would appear on a Saturday, and no one was sure which daughter they were courting.

"My mother talked so much about her home in Odessa, I can visualize it. There was their large living-dining room with six windows running the length of it and a long carpeted table in the middle on which stood the steaming samovar. It was there that my grandfather received his visitors on weekday evenings and the suitors on Saturday. The room also served as a chess parlor. Now, where was I?"

"Why your mother had trouble getting married."

"Well, as I said, there were no dowries. But, at the same time, the family was extremely proud. A bad combination. My mother may have been the proudest of all the sisters. She had, apparently, always suffered flickers of jealousy, deeply suppressed, at all her younger sisters who had, one by one, stolen her parents' love from her. As she reached the terrible age of thirty, the flickers burst into flame.

"Here they were all married, while she, the oldest daughter, had no husband! And she was not only the most beautiful and talented but had been the most giving, the most self-sacrificing of all the daughters! What had she not done for her family? She deserved the best husband of all! I don't think that feeling ever left her, Bernie."

"Had she really been so self-sacrificing?"

"I think so. I'm not sure. The details may come to me later. What I do remember is her telling me proudly that her father thought so highly of her, that he quashed every romance of hers. No one was good enough for her!"

"Was she only proud? I wonder how she really felt about that."

"Good point. I never thought of that. She worshipped her father and spoke of him only in glowing terms. But she must have had mixed feelings. Anyway, then she saw someone who took up two years of her time and left her waiting at the altar."

"A fourteen carat cad. So, how did she meet your father?"

"Through a fluke. You might say a miracle. One day during her rebound period, Dvorah's younger brother Hershel turned up bursting with news. But before I tell you this news, I have to fill you in on some history. We're talking about the mid twenties, after the Russian Revolution. Conditions were such that Jews were leaving the country in droves. Dvorah's father had made a firm decision to emigrate with his family to Palestine as soon as all the members of his family could obtain passports and so forth. I'm sure you know the Soviets made emigration extremely difficult.

"At a meeting of the clandestine zionist organization, Hershel had become friendly with an enterprising young man who for two years had been the Secretary General of the new Jewish Community Council the Soviets had set up in Kiev for Jews, as one of the U.S.S.R.'s many nationalities. From this position, he had been able to create false passports for hundreds of Jews eager to leave the Soviet Union, mostly without remuneration since most Jews were so poor. Unfortunately, the Soviets eventually traced the source of these false passports. Now wanted as a counter-revolutionary, he had fled Kiev and was living under an alias in Odessa."

"Let me guess what happened next. He offered some passports to Hershel for his family."

"You're almost right. This young man, Abraham, quite logically had helped himself to one of the false passports and had also created one for his 'wife' although he didn't have a wife. Again, in the hope of helping someone else. He was offering his services to Hershel who was quite a bit shorter than he. If Hershel wished, he could put on a babushka and join him as his 'wife' when he left Odessa the next day. After a sleepless night, Hershel decided the venture was too risky. He suggested his sister, my mother, take his place.

"My mother told me sardonically how Hershel broached the idea. His eyes had twinkled. 'Abraham's a charmer, Dvorah. Well-spoken. As good-hearted as they come. And he's a guy who always knows all the angles. Always lands on his feet. Do you know, at the age of twenty-four, under the Soviets, he was already the manager of one of the largest banks in Kiev? Believe me. You could do a lot worse.'"

"Hershel and her father, Noah, escorted Dvorah to meet Abraham on a Wednesday morning. Dvorah, overwhelmed at the rapid turn of events, was pleasantly surprised by Abraham's good looks and bearing. He appeared delighted with hers. My uncle Hershel later told me he sensed an electric current between them.

"With Noah's blessing, Dvorah and Abraham left for Volochisk, a border town on a river between Russia and Rumania, where they could wait for an opportunity to cross. Since Volochisk was over-flowing with Jews waiting to flee the U.S.S.R., it might take weeks or even months.

"Nobody has ever told me what transpired between them in Volochisk. But, from the knowing glances my parents exchanged over the years whenever the name came up, the tender inward smile on my father's face, I can surmise.

"What I do know is that shortly afterward, Noah, still in Odessa, received a beautiful letter in poetic Hebrew from Abraham. It said, 'A short time ago, you gave into my safekeeping a very great treasure. I beg your permission to keep that treasure with me always.'"

"How did your father know poetic Hebrew?"

"Oh, I didn't tell you? He came from a very wealthy family that had lost its money. That's a story in itself. But, as a young boy, he had had excellent tutors, and then he went to a good Yeshiva.

"Noah was very happy that Dvorah, who he had thought

would surely remain an old maid, now had an opportunity to marry a man so highly recommended by Hershel, a man who seemed to value her so much and, moreover, could express himself so eloquently in Hebrew. The fact that she was over thirty and had no dowry must have been a factor. At any rate, he gave his prompt assent.

"My parents married immediately. They apparently used the rhythm method. But my mother was misinformed and picked the wrong time of the month as the 'safe' time. To their bewilderment, I was conceived immediately."

Bernie kissed my forehead and ruffled my hair. "I'll have to remember to thank her for her mistake."

"My parents were very happy for their first few months together. But, as the date of my mother's confinement approached, she became more and more petrified of leaving Russia to have the baby 'all alone somewhere among strangers'. She insisted on giving birth at home in the bosom of her family, on familiar sheets.

"So, instead of crossing the frozen river and emigrating at once as they had originally planned, they returned to Odessa a few weeks before I was due."

"They actually went back to Odessa?"

"Yes. Now, for the first time, her family met my father. And Noah, the patriarch, who had only met Abraham once and briefly, took this splendid opportunity to judge his new son-in-law's character."

"Poor Abraham," Bernie said.

"Precisely. I never knew what transpired during those few weeks. All I know is that nothing was ever the same between Dvorah and Abraham after that. It's as if something went awry for them at that moment, and all the king's horses and all the king's men could never put it together again."

"And then you were born?"

"Prematurely. At the worst possible moment."

"Why the worst possible moment?"

"Because I was born during this fight or whatever it was my

parents had, so that they never had the opportunity to work out whatever it was that had come between them."

"I gather, being an exceptionally bright baby, you immediately assessed the situation in the Soviet Union and urged your parents to get out fast."

"Yes. Besides, my father was a wanted man. Having lost their earlier opportunity to emigrate, my father now had to devise some new strategy. True to form, he did.

"Before I was six weeks old, my mother, father and I had left Odessa for Istanbul."

"Now you've lost me, Zvi. Why Istanbul?"

"Well, you see, as I said, my mother's family to whom she was deeply attached were just about to emigrate to Palestine. My mother longed with every fiber of her being to join them there.

"But my father adamantly refused. What he wanted was to join his mother and sister in New York. This did not make much sense since the American quota for Russians had closed in 1924, and this was 1927. The best he could hope for was to be on the same continent with them in Canada. But, of course, he did have a powerful attachment to his mother. He was her only son, and she had always lived for him. Now where was I?"

"Why they went to Istanbul."

"Well, Istanbul was a compromise for both my parents. They spent three whole years there, the three crucial years of their marriage and my infancy, fighting out this cardinal problem of their lives."

"Do you remember anything about your life in Istanbul?"

"No. I know just what my father told me. Since he was in his glory there, he has talked about it endlessly to me. Also, my mother threw up to my father innumerable times that from the moment I was born, I became his child, and he felt no child had ever been born like me. He named me Zviah, after his father, Zvi - a saint, according to my father. Zvi supported all the poor, Jewish and Gentile, in his town. Every girl who needed a dowry, etc. He loved everyone, and everyone loved him. And from the start, my father claimed he saw all his father's virtues in me."

"Okay. So you were named after his saintly father."

"What else do I know about Istanbul? Oh, like so many babies there, I developed a severe case of dysentery and would have died as so many did, had it not been for my father. He carried me around in the palm of his hand - he later demonstrated this - from doctor to doctor with tears in his eyes. The Istanbul doctors hooted with laughter. Babies got dysentery and died. That was the way of the world. You try again next year. In desperation, my father began to meet every boat that docked. Maybe he'd find a European doctor on vacation. Finally, he succeeded. He managed to locate a French doctor who provided a medicine unknown in Turkey. My life was saved.

"My father's reward was that when I began to walk, I walked straight to him. And when, at the age of a year and a half, I choked on a piece of apple, my first cry was not 'Mama' but 'Papa'!"

"How do you know all this?"

"My father has told me dozens of times."

"I don't understand something, Zvi. Wasn't your father working?"

"Sure. I told you, didn't I? He had a great job as Comptroller of the Turkish Steamship Lines. He was in charge of exchanging French currency for British currency, etc."

"Was your mother working?"

"Of course not. My father was doing extremely well. We had a beautiful apartment."

"Then, here's what I don't understand. Why was it your father who was taking you to doctors? What happened to your mother?"

I felt my face working. "I don't know."

"I mean, did she refuse to take you? Is that why your father took over?"

"Bernie, I don't know."

"Or were they competing for you, and he won?"

"I wish I knew. Clearly, he did take over. But I've never

been able to figure out why. Whether he grew attached to me because she was so cold to him. Or if she grew cold to him because he seemed to have transferred his love from her to me. Does that make sense? Sometimes I had the feeling she saw me as the 'other woman' who was out to steal her husband. Crazy, isn't it?"

"A one year old 'other woman'."

"Bernie, I never knew if, since she was giving me so little love, he felt he had to compensate. Or if, since he was giving me so much and he and I had such a strong attachment, she was jealous. It's been the central enigma of my life."

"You have no clues?"

"I'd give my right arm to get some. All I know is, I'm sure she never kissed me or hugged me or said an affectionate word to me. And I never knew why..." I felt my voice breaking.

"Poor Zvi. And even in therapy no memories came up?"

"My therapist, Amos, was wonderful for me. He helped me detach from my mother so that very little she can do now upsets me. And he helped me get over my anger and make peace with myself so I could get on with my life. And, believe me, I was very eager to get on with my life. I was already in my late thirties, and if I didn't remarry soon, there was a good chance I'd never remarry. So we both chose not to continue the way some therapists do for eighteen years working everything out. And there are some things I didn't have the answers to. Bernie, I really don't want to talk about this."

"I'm sorry if I upset you by probing. Tell you what. Let's go have some hot chocolate. With whipped cream. That cures most ills."

I relaxed over the hot chocolate.

"I might as well finish up with Istanbul."

"If you're sure you want to."

"This part's okay. A short time after our arrival, my mother's whole family passed on their way to Palestine. Since they had a two hour stop-over, my parents were, naturally, there to meet them at the dock. My mother's father, Noah, begged and pleaded with my father to join them in Palestine. You must remember how arrogant this grandfather of mine was. My mother, who revered him, was deeply touched that he should 'grovel' in that way before her husband.

"This time my father was prepared for his father-in-law.

"Dressed in his best, even to his spats, my father was courteous and properly deferential, almost bowing from the waist, that seat of politeness. But, in the gentlest possible terms, he categorically refused to go to Palestine. This time, his excuse was that life in Palestine was not safe. Hadn't the Arabs recently massacred all the Jews of Hebron? Abraham had been through too many pograms already and couldn't face more stress. This, of course, was also true. Several members of his family had been killed, as a matter of fact, and he, himself, had almost lost his life more than once.

"My father veered between these excuses for the rest of his life and gave no inkling of any other reason for refusing to live in Palestine - later Israel.

"My parents wrangled over this issue for another two and a half years. Day and night.

"In the end, my father won. When I was three years and two months old, we set sail for Canada.

"My mother knew she'd never see her beloved family again and didn't stop crying for the entire thirteen days of the trip. She lay seasick in her cabin. She also stopped eating.

"On October 14, 1930, my mother, father and I arrived in Montreal - a Montreal in the throes of the Depression."

It was later in bed, when Bernie and I lay snuggled against each other that I burst out, "Bernie, you won't believe this! But I do have a memory of Istanbul."

"You do?"

"In fact, I have two memories. But they're just the barest fragments. They don't connect to anything."

"Go ahead. I'm all ears."

"I wish I could attach them to something. The first is of legs. Women's legs. Women's bare legs. And feet. What do you make of that?"

"From which angle are you seeing them?"

"From down by the floor."

"That's easy. You're a baby playing among grown up feet."

"Hey! You're great! But what puzzles me is how come I was in a house with so many women! My parents didn't know anyone in Istanbul."

Bernie thought a moment. "That I don't know. What's the second memory?"

"That's even more of a fragment. It's just of being high up somewhere."

"Like on a swing?"

"No. Like on a hill." My mind struggled for more details. "Oh, well, maybe it's something I saw in a movie."

"Sweetie, why don't we get some sleep, huh?"

But the floodgates were open again. The memories I had so carefully folded away returned.

Part 2

Reliving Canada

Chapter 3

My years in Montreal were like a toothache. I managed to survive them only by numbing myself against the pain.

My most piercing memories remained blocked and buried for decades. Until I went into therapy with Amos.

But there were some things I remembered vividly. I remembered my mother's screaming at my father.

"*Vu host tu mich farshlept?* Where did you drag me to?" My mother's voice shrilled through the nights and down the years. "I had a family! A father who was somebody! Brothers who were respected. A house always full of the finest people! Here, you're a nobody so I'm a nobody, too! You tore me away from my family! From my own flesh and blood! And you buried me alive! Since we've been here, there hasn't been a day that I haven't had to worry would there be food on the table! And for this you dragged me all the way to your godforsaken Canada," she placed the accent on the second syllable, "where we don't have a single brother or sister." Her voice rose. "Where we're *ingantzen alein!*"

"Alein", alone, was the most terrible word in the Yiddish language.

On our bookcase stood a permanent reminder of my mother's origins, sent us by her family from Palestine shortly after our arrival in Montreal. An olivewood camel kneeling on a small platform. In the camel's hump was imbedded an inkwell. The olivewood cover to this inkwell contained a deep notch into which fitted an elaborately carved olivewood pen. The widest part of this pen had a hole through it, covered by a magnifying glass. When you looked into this glass, you saw a sunny Jerusalem.

As a little girl, I found myself peering into that magnifying glass often. I desperately needed to know a sunnier life existed somewhere.

For life in Montreal was grim.

My parents had arrived in Montreal totally unaware of its

social structure.

Montreal is beautiful, and my parents at first were entranced by its physical charms. On the western slopes of Mt. Royal, in Westmount, the stone mansions of the very rich, the English and Scotch, climbed the leafy, winding streets, each house set like a jewel atop its terraced garden.

But, in another orbit at the very foot of the mountain, lay the immigrant Jewish section, called by Saul Bellow the worst ghetto this side of Czarist Russia. It stretched from Pine Avenue on the south almost to Van Horne on the north; from a little beyond Main Street on the east to a few blocks past Park Avenue on the west. Here, dingy tenements stood row upon row, all with identical long, drab wooden staircases leading up to the second and third stories. Here, in winter, parents got up in the dark to carry coal from rat infested rear sheds to make fires in cast iron stoves so their children would wake to a warm house. Here, so many men couldn't make a living in the only ways open to them, hawking fruit or vegetables or bread rolls from rented wagons, that most families subsisted only because the wives also worked, climbing hundreds of ice-covered stairs in winter to sell hand sewn aprons or children's clothes or potholders to compassionate neighbors only a little less poor than themselves.

No Gentile firm would hire a Jew. Nor would the government. Whole industries were, therefore, barred to us. Later, during the war, Jews weren't even accepted in war plants fighting Hitler!

The passport out of the Lower East Side of New York had been education. But, here in Montreal, Jews needed much higher grades to get into either of the two English speaking colleges. Moreover, there was no free college. People starved themselves and kept boarders for years to enable one son to attend McGill University.

Each time I took a streetcar with my father who had a pronounced Yiddish accent, the French streetcar conductor was sure to intone, "Get to the rear of the car, *maudit Juif.* - Damn Jew."

When we first arrived, my father had gone into the lubricating oil business with a "landsman", a man from his village of Vorrini. Velvel came from a family so lowly, he had arrived in Canada without a surname. My mother couldn't tolerate his crassness.

"He has fingers like sausages!" she cringed.

Look what her husband had brought her down to! And her Abraham was able to make only the most paltry of livings by selling stinking oil and coming home with disgusting greasy hands with black under his fingernails.

Soon Dvorah didn't have to worry about Velvel. He decided to become a butcher and leave the worthless oil business to Abraham.

Personally, I have never understood how my father was able to make any kind of living out of the lubricating oil business. After all, this was the Depression, and nobody in the ghetto had a car! How much could he possibly earn selling a thimbleful of oil for sewing machines!

My father had been able to cope with all the convolutions of the Russian Revolution and land on his feet. He had succeeded beautifully in a totally foreign country with a new language, new culture, and new mores. Turkey. But the Montreal ghetto during the Depression was beyond even his capabilities.

As he constantly said, "How can you succeed in a country where you don't know where a door opens?" All his charisma and charm and talents went for naught here.

Still, despite the almost insuperable difficulties encountered by my father, as long as my mother showed some faith in him, he worked endless hours against every discouragement.

All this changed the day my brother was born.

What happened was this.

My mother, who had always felt I was my father's child and not hers, desperately wanted a child of her own. When I was four, therefore, she bore my brother Mitch, whom she named after her father's father, Moishe, the *Agaon* of Czernowitz. She identified Mitch with her family so much that in absent-minded moments, she often called Mitch "Dovid" after her older, much-admired brother, something that infuriated Mitch more and more as he grew older. He considered the parallel a millstone around his neck.

He became the center of her life. She lived only for and

through him. She almost completely supplanted her husband with her son, totally unaware that she was exactly following her hated mother-in-law's pattern.

Up to this point, my father's discouragement had been largely due to external circumstances beyond his control. Now, he began to lose the remains of his incentive. He stayed in bed late, leaving it to his wife to make up the two coal stoves each day so *he* could wake to a warm house.

My mother could not have been more bitter.

"When you *schlepped* me here, and God knows coming here was the last thing on earth I wanted to do, I, at the very least, thought we'd get rich. Everyone I ever knew or even heard of got rich in America. That, in addition to being a nobody, you shouldn't even be able to feed your family is something I never in my wildest nightmares imagined! You were always boasting what a big shot you were in Russia. Some big shot! What kind of person can't make a living in America?"

That there was a Depression in America, in Canada, in fact, over much of the world, was something she never quite grasped.

From her vast arsenal of abuse, my mother selected a few choice epithets each day to describe my father's worthlessness. *Lo-itzlach*, a word of Hebrew derivation meaning one who does not succeed but connotating a clumsy oaf, was the mildest of them.

Gradually, as water wears away a stone, her barrage eroded his confidence which had been based on such a firm foundation of achievements in Soviet Russia and Istanbul.

And so began the cycle.

My mother denigrated my father for being lazy and good-for-nothing.

My father refused to make an effort against such odds for a wife who not only didn't value him but brought him so little happiness.

Therefore, my mother denigrated him all the more for being lazy and good-for-nothing.

Therefore he refused to make an effort....

To add to my mother's bitterness, there was Abraham's mother. She arrived around the time of the baby's birth ostensibly to "help" her and was supposed to stay six weeks but remained for a year and a half. She set the tone very early in her stay. The night my mother gave birth to Mitch, I heard my grandmother say to our neighbor, "My poor Avrameleh! What he went through last night! He didn't sleep a wink!"

She further incensed my mother by bringing Abraham his breakfast in bed; cooking special foods for him because presumably his wife didn't know how to look after his delicate stomach; greeting him at the door with a warm glass of milk in her hand on the rare winter days when he did venture out to make sales, and, in general, commiserating with how hard her Avrameleh was working for his wife.

Chapter 4

My parents were both proud of not assimilating into Canadian life. Like the Bourbon kings of old, they learned nothing and forgot nothing.

This, of course, made it difficult to make friends.

But my mother, especially, would have disdained to make friends with anyone whose background was not as fine as hers. Therefore, while she was very lonely, her loneliness was more than partly of her own choosing.

At long last, needing company badly, she found an organization which met some of her requirements. The Pioneer Women not only raised money for Palestine, but also provided Jewish cultural programs of a high caliber.

Here, Dvorah was in her element and, while still having difficulty with making personal friends, quickly rose to being president of the Montreal chapter.

When I was about seven and a half, this group decided to give a Chanuka party that would consist of a concert with home grown talent. Now, finally, my mother had her opportunity to shine. She offered to be the solo singer. She had an immense repertoire of Hebrew and Jewish songs and would be delighted to perform them. It was the high point of her life in Montreal up to now, and she prepared for this concert for weeks. Not only did she rehearse her songs, but she sewed herself a black velvet dress she copied from a pattern in a magazine. With this dress, she would wear the amber beads Abraham had bought her just before they left Istanbul. The beads were beautiful and exotic, and she was more than happy to show them off.

But Dvorah was excited about this evening for yet another reason. The guest speaker would be Chaim G___, one of the world's foremost Zionists, the editor of Hebrew and Zionist periodicals and now living in the United States. He was, in addition, an old friend of her brother, Dovid, from the Odessa days, which in itself gave him an aura beyond that of any ordinary mortal. Since he was the guest speaker and she the principal and solo performer and, since he had known her brother, they would surely be thrown together! Finally, *finally* she would be in the company of a somebody!

My mother talked of nothing else for weeks, totally unaware of the reaction this was arousing in my father.

On the appointed day, my mother fed the children early, dressed carefully, and waited for my father to return from his rounds. Unfortunately, precisely on this day, so he said, it turned out he had several deliveries to make.

Usually, Abraham was home by five. Now, it was already seven, and he was still not back. What could have happened to him? Now it was nearly eight! My mother waited and waited. And waited. My father did not come home. No one had heard of baby sitters in those days. And she could not leave the children alone.

She sat there hour after hour, her blood slowly turning to ice.

My father did not appear till eleven thirty. He never explained. Had he been jealous of Chaim G____, the world famous Zionist, who was a "somebody" and whom Dvorah was so eager to meet?

When Abraham, finally, walked into the house, an explosion of fury went off in Dvorah's head. She began to scream. She did not stop screaming at him till morning by which time she had completely lost her voice.

Years later, she told me that after that night, each time Abraham lay down next to her in bed, a shiver of revulsion rippled through her.

Having screamed all that night, she then retreated into a glacial silence for the next thirty years.

She broke this silence only upon extraordinary occasions.

One of these occasions occurred six months later when I was eight. To my father's bewilderment, she sat down opposite him at the dinner table one night. Her teeth were clenched.

"I have to speak to you." My father looked stunned. "We have to face it, Abraham," she said. "Zviah will never be pretty. She has dull brown hair. And it's straight. She'll never be pretty as I was. We'll just have to find the money to give her piano lessons."

She made this all important pronouncement to my father in my presence as though I was not there and couldn't hear her. And with no thought as to how it was affecting me.

My father nodded numbly.

Thereafter, a beat up piano we certainly couldn't afford appeared, and a beat up music teacher turned up twice a week to give me lessons. She charged twenty-five cents a lesson.

I kept checking in the mirror. Was it helping? But I looked no prettier. I would never be pretty like my mother. And I certainly was making no progress on the piano.

"What's the matter with her?" asked my mother harshly of my teacher. "Why can't she learn anything?"

Miss Kruger smiled and shrugged. She was not about to jeopardize her fifty cents a week.

My mother nodded sadly. "She has no talent. Right? Don't be afraid to tell me. Zviah can't sing either. I had a wonderful mezzo soprano as a girl. I used to sing in the Odessa Synagogue Choir. You've heard of it?"

"No, Mrs. Berman. I'm afraid I -"

"I was selected out of ninety-six contestants. But she's inherited none of my talents. I was the most musical of all seven sisters. And the prettiest! I had such beautiful curly black hair! Now it's getting grey. But you should have seen it!"

Miss Kruger smiled. She kept coming for another two years. But neither my looks nor my piano playing improved. Miss Kruger gave me lots of Hayden to play, and I began to feel guilty because I massacred so many of his beautiful pieces.

* * * *

"You mean to say she's only eleven, and already she wears a larger size than I do?" My mother and I were in Hirsch's Shoe store on Park Avenue.

"Well, looks like she needs a seven."

"But that's terrible! She can grow and grow. Men hate women with big feet. I wear only a three and a half!"

"Well, maybe girls are growing larger feet these days. You want these shoes for her? How do they feel, dear? Are they comfortable?"

"They're okay."

"Imagine!" exploded my mother. "A seven and she's not yet twelve years old. I thought you'd have tiny feet like mine. I had the smallest feet of all seven sisters."

Apparently, I was not only ugly and unmusical but big and clumsy into the bargain. Was there any hope for me?

* * * *

"What are you doing in my kitchen, Zviah?"

"I thought I'd make lunch for Pa. You were busy with Mitch."

"Oh, so you were doing me a favor! That's nice!"

"Yes. I thought I'd help you. You're always complaining...."

"That's some favor you did me! You burned the stew. Now I have to scour the pan. Besides, lamb stew is not for frying. Whoever heard of fried lamb stew? A stew you stew! You wasted our dinner. I really pity the husband who falls into your hands. He won't stay with you for twenty minutes. I want you out of my kitchen, understand? It's my kitchen and no one but I cook in it. It's not your job to cook for your father. Besides, every time you're in here you make such a mess I have twice as much work cleaning up after you."

"Then why don't you teach me how to cook?"

"Teach you! What's the point of teaching you anything? You're as hopeless in the kitchen as you were on the piano. A fortune we spent on you for two whole years, and you can't play a single piece."

I was ugly. I was unmusical. I was big and clumsy. I had awful hair. I lacked every social grace. I was also totally inept in the kitchen. No man would stay with me more than twenty minutes.

Did I have any virtues at all to hang a hat on? Well, maybe I had one.

I was an excellent student.

* * * *

"You're going to have to leave school," my mother informed me a few days after I had completed my second year of high school.

"What are you talking about? I love school."

"What you love has nothing to do with it. If you don't leave school and get a job, there's no way Moishe will be able to go to college. What's more important?"

"Ma, I get all A's!"

"Nonsense. You're in a stupid class so you get A's. You have no competition. What good would high school do you, anyway? You can get working papers in a few months when you're fourteen and start making money."

"But, Ma, I want to go to college."

"You're talking rubbish. You're not smart enough to go to college, and you know it. What a waste of time! Besides, men hate educated women. You'll never get married. It's a thousand times more important that Moishe go to college so he can have a career. You don't want Moishe to be a luftmensch and live on air like your father without being able to make a living for his family, do you?"

"But, Ma, what about me?"

"You'll get your working papers like all the other girls. You'll work five years and get married at nineteen. Your husband will support you. The subject is closed."

"But, Ma...."

"Do you ever think of anyone but yourself? I never saw anyone so selfish. Do you know when I was a girl, I brought home every cent I earned to my father untouched. So did all my sisters. The money went for our brothers' education as it should. But you? You think only of Zviah."

I waited at the corner till my father came home and poured all my troubles out to him. Lately, he had been so distraught and distant. It was as if he no longer lived with us. But when he heard my story his face started to work.

He immediately began to talk to my mother who, as usual, greeted him grimly.

"Dvorah, Zviah tells me you want to pull her out of school?"

She raised her chin. "So?"

"Dvorah, Zviah gets very high grades. She's so enthusiastic about school. It's her whole life."

"It's high time you both came down to earth. She has to leave school and go to work. Otherwise, there's no way Moishe can go to college. Who's going to support him? You?"

My father reddened.

"Why can't you go to work, Ma? You're a Hebrew teacher."

I was amazed at my brazenness. I had never talked back to her before.

"A chutzpah! I should go to work so she can stay in school! Did you ever hear such a chutzpah?"

"Dvorah, Zviah has a keen mind. She's a thinking person. She needs...."

"Don't you dare tell me what your darling Zviah needs. Moishe is worth ten of Zviah."

"Dvorah, I hate to say this. But I mean it with all my heart. Zviah's worth a hundred of Moishe. She's sensitive -"

My mother turned purple. Her eyes glinted. "Listen, you! Get out of my house if you don't like the way I raise the children! I never want to see you here again!"

"Dvorah," my father spoke softly. "Try to see reason. Once she drops out of school, there'll be no turning back. And what kind of job could she get at this point? She'll be stuck in a factory for life."

"You'd sell us all for Zviah. It's always been that way. I still remember Istanbul. She's leaving school. And that's that. Besides, she's not smart enough for college. I already told her. She wasn't even smart enough to learn to play the piano after two whole years. You see in her what you want to see. She's not smart enough for high school either. Especially not an academic high school that teaches her nothing practical. How's winning an English medal going to put food on anyone's table? Tell me that. Why throw away ten dollars a month on school fees? Next year it'll be fifteen. I can think of lots more important things to do with the money. Ten dollars grows on trees?"

Who was right? My father or my mother? Was I really smart enough to go to college?

Still, I went on a hunger strike. It wasn't easy. I was so hungry I couldn't sleep nights. I became weak and trembly. But I stuck it out. And, although my father kept trying to sneak food to me, I didn't cheat.

After I hadn't eaten for five days, and my father kept battering my mother, we finally won.

Or rather they struck a compromise.

I was to be allowed to go to high school. But - I'd have to earn every penny of my school tuition.

Since I could only earn a quarter an hour working at the Five and Dime, and, since in the fourth year the fees went up to twenty dollars a month, that meant I also had to tutor every spare moment to earn the tuition money.

I still loved high school. But it became a treadmill.

Despite all the hours of work I put in outside of school, I kept up my grades by studying long hours on Sunday and into the nights. A paper I wrote on the humor and wisdom in "As You Like It," won another medal. A painting I did won a schoolwide contest and was permanently hung in the Assembly. School was the one place where I won approval. Where I shone. It was my refuge.

Yet, somehow, my success there did not change my self concept. My mother denigrated school. Therefore, it could not be important. And maybe she was right. Maybe I stood out only because I had no competition. My mother had also dinned into me the fact that for a girl to get high grades was not only not an asset, it was a distinct liability. Yet another liability!

In addition to all this, my mother never forgave me. Forever after, I was to be the evil, selfish daughter.

"You don't know the kind of person she is," I heard her tell neighbors.

* * * *

Late one night, when I was about fourteen, I had just sunk into a tub to relax when my mother, suddenly, walked into the bathroom. For a moment, she stared with popping eyes at my large breasts that protruded from the water with a look of what I could only call horror. Why the horror? I searched her face. But that was, apparently, precisely what she wanted to avoid - my knowing what I would see if I could look into her soul. She hurriedly left the room.

Why had my mother been so horrified at seeing my breasts? There could be only one answer. She was ashamed of them. I absorbed the shame of my female body, and it became part of me.

I used to hate our black serge school uniform thinking it had been conceived by people just like my mother to hide the breasts of growing girls. Now I began to see it as a godsend. In fact, over it, I started to wear a loose cardigan to make sure no one could possibly see my breasts. So men would not whistle at me on the street.

Despite all this concealment, a handsome, popular boy, Kenny Siegel, inexplicably invited me to the Junior Prom.

The war was on. In Canada, we had conscription which created a dreadful male shortage all the way down to our age level. The girls in my high school class, all miles more mature than I was sexually and emotionally, competed in the most intense way for the few "worthwhile" boys that remained.

The day the word got out that I had a date with no less a personage than Kenny Siegel, my classroom was buzzing.

"You'll never guess who has a date for the Junior Prom with Kenny! Sylvia Berman!"

"I don't believe it!"

I couldn't believe it, either.

In fact, I was so overwhelmed at the honor of dating Kenny whom every girl in my class was after that I spent weeks prior to the dance memorizing witty comments with which to hold his interest.

But, even as I culled and wrote down these gems, I knew in my heart that all my efforts would be for naught. Hadn't my mother told me time and time again that I was stupid, that I never knew how to talk to people? Even ordinary people! Let alone someone as special as Kenny who could afford to be choosey!

I worked myself up into such a pitch the evening of the Prom that I couldn't utter a single word to Kenny. He left me for another girl. It was the worst evening of my life!

* * * *

I remember being miserable and depressed during all these years. I saw the world as a place impossible to be happy in. I am told I was cynical. I may have been more than a little sullen. But I was not really angry. Perhaps I thought all mothers were like mine.

The anger came much later.

But the seed may have been sown the day I met the mother of a new girlfriend, Mira. Mira was, everyone thought, just average in appearance. But her mother didn't think so. Once when I was visiting her, Mira came into the living room all dressed up, wearing high heels. Her mother turned to me with a glow.

"I tell you my Miraleh is *azoy schoen as meh can hier in ponem nit cooken*." "I tell you people are so dazzled by my Mirahleh's beauty that they can't look her in the face."

Tears sprang to my eyes. I was astonished. Then, all mothers were not like mine!

But, again, I quickly buried the feeling.

Chapter 5

My father began to suffer stomach spasms. To the extreme annoyance of my mother who could think of a hundred more important things to do with the money, his doctor became a frequent visitor.

Dr. Rabinowitz was a figure out of a Gay Nineties cartoon. He spoke from under a grey bushy mustache and wore a pince nez. The heavy chain of a large gold watch gleamed across his vested soft round belly. He always came carrying a tiny Chihuahua in his plump arms. Since, like my father, he was also a Biblical scholar, which was what they had in common, he had named the dog Nebuchadnezzer.

Dr. Rabinowitz loved my father. Each time he arrived, he shut himself up with him in my father's tiny office and talked to him for hours, all for the same two dollars. Quite a tribute to my father's company.

One day, when I was home sick, they were discussing the fact that my father's problem was psychosomatic, although, at that time, the term was unknown. I clearly heard my father make a heart-wrenching confession.

"Dr. Rabinowitz, what do you do when you have a cold wife and a blooming daughter?" I was perhaps fourteen at the time.

"Abe, don't be a *yold*," Dr. Rabinowitz's cynical laugh rang through the door. "You get another woman, that's what you do. I get around. Once in a while I hear of someone - you know, someone who's bored with her husband." I could just see Dr. Rabinowitz leer.

He, himself, had been through three marriages and was known as quite a womanizer.

"Wait, I do know of someone!"

I heard my father gasp. "I'm not that kind of person, doctor."

"Everyone's that kind of person," the doctor laughed. "Don't be so high and mighty."

"I can't live that way," my father said primly. "I can't sneak around. How would it look? I have nice children."

"I also know some good whorehouses. Clean ones. Remember, I'm a doctor for a few of them."

"Dr. Rabinowitz, please," my father sounded revolted.

"All right." I heard the scrape of Dr. Rabinowitz's chair which meant he was getting up to leave. "Have it your way. You told me your problem. I offered a solution. Now you suit yourself."

* * * *

My father, like his father, gained great satisfaction from helping others, so instead of following the doctor's advice, he threw his energies into helping the Goldstein family, distant relatives of one of his aunts in Russia.

Rabbi Goldstein had been killed in a pogrom in Warsaw some years ago, and Mrs. Goldstein and her children had immigrated to Canada. Since the only immigrants Canada was accepting at the time were farmers, this city bred family declared themselves to be farmers and were granted a desolate piece of land some miles north of Winnipeg. As soon as they could, they sold it and migrated to the nearest city with a large Jewish population, Montreal, in the midst of the Depression, not knowing which way to turn.

My father bent every effort to find them a place where they could afford to live and even succeeded in doing the almost impossible, securing a stenographic job for the daughter, Alice. Neither of her younger brothers could find work, and her mother was unemployable. Alice, a brilliant woman in her early thirties, had not only overcome her accent and mastered English, but, within a very few years, had turned herself into an excellent legal secretary and had taken on the support of her entire family.

The fact that their father had been a rabbi in Poland, descended from a long line of rabbis, made Alice and her mother more or less acceptable to my mother, and they became family friends. Once in a while, Alice even brought her best friend, Edith, a charming, educated woman, who was Alice's boss's sister and also a legal secretary in the same office.

One Friday afternoon near the end of my last year of high school, as I hurried from school to tutor the first of my two pupils of the day, I was surprised to find my father waiting for me at the school gate. Somehow, he looked different.

I ran up to him.

"Papa, what happened?"

My father appeared happy yet agonized at the same time.

"Ketzeleh, I just wanted to tell you I won't be home for dinner."

"For this you came to school?"

He smiled. "It's a bit more complicated than that."

"What? Tell me."

He took a deep breath and met my eyes. "I won't be home tonight, either."

"I don't understand."

He said nothing but his face crumpled as he stared at me. His large eyes brimmed with tears.

"You broke up with Ma!"

"God bless you, Ketzeleh. You're so smart."

My stomach flipped. "Oh, Papa. For good?" I would lose my Papa and have no protector at all! I couldn't bear that! "Oh, Papa, you wouldn't do that to me! You wouldn't leave me! Please don't leave me! Please Papa!"

"It's all right." His face had changed again. Now he was smiling broadly. It was as if the sun had come out. "It's all right, Ketzeleh. You have nothing to worry about. I'm staying with another woman. A very fine woman. You know her."

"I know her? Who?"

"Eda"

"You meant Edith." I smiled. My father had never mastered the English "th". But, if he had come to share all this with me, then he wasn't about to leave me. I breathed easier. "Alice's friend, Edith?"

He nodded.

So many emotions raced through me.

First, I was bewildered. I couldn't understand how a Canadian born woman who spoke English so beautifully and came from a wealthy assimilated family that had lost its money would accept an immigrant like my father who couldn't even pronounce her name. It spoke very well for his charm and the warmth of his personality.

Then, I was delighted for him. It was high time he knew some happiness.

Suddenly, I was also very happy and excited for myself. Maybe he would marry Edith, and I'd be able to live with them and get away from my mother!

"Oh, Papa, when you marry her, can I live with you?"

My father smiled. "Not so fast, Ketzeleh. Let's see what develops. These things take time. I had to come and see you because I didn't know what Ma would tell you. I didn't want you to wait and wonder and worry. Or to think I just ran out and forgot you."

"Oh, Papa, I know you'd never do that."

My father smiled again. "Of course, I wouldn't. Zviahleh, I'll meet you here again in a few days. Let's say Tuesday. Maybe then I'll arrange for you to talk to Eda. Would you like that?"

As he uttered the word "Eda" he rolled his tongue lovingly around it, savoring it as though it had a flavor of its own.

"I'd love it."

"You remember her, don't you? She used to visit us with Alice."

"Of course. I think she's very nice."

"So do I! And I think she likes you, too." He looked delighted.

"Oo! I hope she does."

"Of course, Ketzeleh. Don't worry about anything. It'll work out. I'll see you Tuesday. Oh, and be sure to tell Moishe."

* * * *

My mother gently handed Mitch his soup. "How it is, Moisheleh? Not too salty for you?" She stood watching him eat. All through my childhood, my mother never took her eyes off him.

"It's okay," mumbled Mitch. "I just don't like barley soup."

"Oh, I'm sorry. I wish I had known. You should have told me."

"I told you last time. You never listen to anything."

"Moisheleh, listen. I'll make you a potato soup. With leeks. It'll take just twenty minutes."

"Never mind. I'm not hungry anyway."

"What do you mean you're not hungry? You ate no lunch, either. You're not sick, God forbid, are you?"

"I'm not sick. Leave me alone, Ma, will you?"

Then, my mother's demeanor changed dramatically.

She shoved my soup at me as usual. This time, she shoved it so hard it sloshed all over the table. She wiped it up, glaring at me.

"You might as well know, both of you," she announced in a metallic voice. "Your father and I broke up. He left me for a younger woman. The chutzpah! The gall! To drag me all the way out to Canada and...I told him, 'You want to go! Then go! Who needs you, anyway!' Some prize she's getting! I told your father if he ever sets foot in this house again, I'll kill him!"

Mitch and I both stared at her.

"What's going to happen to us?" Mitch asked.

"Nothing'll happen. You'll stay here with me. Zviah, you don't look surprised. Maybe you've known about all this from the start?"

"No, Ma."

"He'd better give me money for the house. That's all I have to say."

I got up from the table. My head ached.

"Where do you think you're going. It never occurred to you to help me with the dishes?

"Ma, I work about a hundred hours a week. I'm exhausted.

Besides, you said you don't want me in the kitchen."

"Do you know when I was a little girl, only seven years old, my mother kept an inn. And every day I had to make not only my bed, but six other beds as well. Only seven years old and I never told my mother I was tired."

"Why don't you get Mitch to help?"

"Mitch? Did you say Mitch? Mitch is a boy. Boys don't belong in the kitchen."

"Ma, I work very long hours. Besides, I have a party to go to tonight. Mira's Sweet Sixteen. I told you." I turned toward the outside door.

"You're going to a party, and that's what you're wearing?"

"What's wrong with it?"

"What makes you think you look good in green?"

My head began to ache more violently.

My mother's face changed as a new thought struck her. "There will be boys there?"

"Of course."

Her voice was sharp, her eyes probing. "You know what going out with boys means?"

She had given me the same lecture the night I went out with Kenny.

"Yes." Although all I knew couldn't fill a thimble.

"Do you know that a boy doesn't respect you if you let him touch you?"

My temple was throbbing. Perhaps I wouldn't go out tonight after all. I was much too tense. It was true I didn't look good in green. Yet, it was the only dressy dress I had.

Chapter 6

I began to visit my father and Edith every Sunday for lunch and to stay all afternoon.

I loved those lunches Edith made for me.

I loved the way she talked to me and the way she listened to me.

"What's your favorite subject in school?" she started. Most adults ask such a question perfunctorily. But she sounded as if she really was interested in the answer. And cared. So I gave her real answers.

"English, most of all. Then, history. And, oh, art. I love Thursdays when we have art."

"What do you think you want to be when you graduate college?"

She had said the magic words "graduate college"! I loved her!

"Well, first I have to get through college, don't I? I'll have to go to Sir George Williams, you know, that little YMCA college, at night. God knows how many years that will take. Eight or nine. And I'm not sure exactly what I want to be. All I know is that I want to go. No. I *have* to go. You know, Edith, it's like I'm following a star!"

Edith smiled warmly as if she understood me completely.

"You sound as if you'd make a great English teacher!"

"My English teacher, Miss Rorke, thinks I'd make a good English teacher. She told me so. And my art teacher thinks I'd make a good art teacher. But they're talking about teaching in High School. I don't know if I have the confidence to handle teenagers or if I'm smart enough. Anyway, Jews can't teach in high school in Montreal, as I'm sure you know."

"No reason you have to stay in Montreal all your life. There's a great shortage of Jewish men here, anyway. There are no opportunities for them so they go elsewhere." She studied me. "New York might be a good place for you. Several million Jews and a much more stimulating atmosphere. And you are smart enough."

It was so easy to talk to her!

Edith lived in Outremont, a much more attractive neighborhood.

I enjoyed seeing my father and Edith together. He seemed completely transformed. I watched him now as the afternoon sunshine, sifted through the foliage outside Edith's window with its patterns of light and shade, lit up his ruddy cheeks, his broad brow, the straight nose that ended in a little square tip. He had lost those tortured lines about his face. He looked tranquil and serene.

As for Edith, she must have been very pretty at one time although now in her early forties, her prettiness had faded. But she was tall, dark blond, slim, well-groomed, even tempered. She wore clothes with a flair. Perhaps she had good classic clothes left over from her wealthy days.

What I liked best about her, however, was the expression in her clear, grey eyes when she looked at my father. And sometimes at me.

My father and Edith held hands a lot and laughed a lot. Suddenly, everything seemed funny. They shared private jokes. She listened raptly when he told his stories.

Each Sunday was like a golden bubble in my life.

* * * *

Unfortunately, it was not to last.

It turned out that Edith had another suitor who was a bachelor and could marry her. Moreover, her other suitor, although a rigid, dull person, not nearly as much fun as my father, had lots of money, and Edith, who had grown up in a wealthy family, hated being poor. She knew she'd remain poor if she married my father who had to support another family.

For some months, she tried to help my father make more money by getting him interested in real estate. She even provided him with wealthy contacts.

"My brother says it's the coming thing. There'll be lots of money to be made in real estate as soon as the veterans come back. I know you'll be good at it."

But she was talking about after the war. This was 1943. Who knew how long the war would last? My father made a valiant attempt to sell real estate to his new contacts. But he had no experience. It was too soon, and he failed.

Edith refused to wait and jeopardize her chances with the other man who demanded an answer. Very reluctantly, she gave my father up.

My father was heartbroken. So was I.

He went back to my mother. One day he turned up at her door, looking haggard.

"Oh, so you're back?" my mother said smugly. "I knew she wouldn't stay with you. *A zah metziah!* Such a bargain!"

*   *   *   *

But his experience with Edith permanently changed my father. He remained buoyant. After that, it was as if nothing my mother said could sting him.

He'd counter with some comment like, "Nu, the sages said that a man who has a wife is blessed because he now has someone to point out his faults to him. I've been just a little more blessed than most."

Edith changed him permanently in yet another way. By having faith in him.

After the war, my father made a fresh attempt to sell real estate. It took him a year or two to learn how. But, using his new contacts which gave him a toehold in the tiny, wealthy Montreal Jewish community, he finally succeeded. He made far more money in 1946 than he had in all previous sixteen years in Montreal.

He continued to be successful. We moved out of our cold-water ghetto flat into a lovely steam-heated apartment in Cote des Neiges, the new neighborhood adjacent to Westmount just beginning to be "infiltrated" by Jews. He bought my mother a beautiful black Persian lamb coat. My mother who had complained so bitterly when he had not made a living, showed no appreciation now that he was doing so well.

Quite the contrary. The very fact that we now had money set off a fresh new cycle of quarrels between them. For the first time, it was possible to fly to Israel, and we could afford it.

"Dvorah, I'll give you the money. You can go. But you can't make me go. And I won't."

On this one issue, I was with my mother. Despite how she treated me, I could feel her loneliness and felt deeply sorry for her. I knew that, if my father went even for the briefest visit, she would stop holding this club against him, and we'd all find her easier to live with.

I also knew, however, that while I could ask my father almost anything else and he'd answer, I couldn't ask him why he refused to go to Israel.

"Murderer!" Her eyes blazed. "You have the heart of a murderer! You know I'm dying to see my family, and you're killing me!"

"Ma," I ventured. "I know how much you long to see all of them. How lonely you are. Why don't you go alone?"

She turned on me with venom. "Because if I go alone, I'll be announcing to them that my marriage is a failure. That my life is a failure! I can't go alone! And he knows it!"

She never did!

*　*　*　*

In the meantime, in the four years since my high school graduation, I had been attending Sir George Williams College at night, where, to my astonishment, I was achieving excellent grades although I had no hope of ever graduating. By day, I worked at such mind-stifling jobs I thought I'd go mad.

One day in the summer of 1946, my father called me into his tiny office. "Zviahleh," his face was wreathed in smiles, "now you can go to McGill full time!"

The earth swung around me. "What?"

"I mean it. I can now afford it. Now you can go to McGill!"

It was as though he had handed me the sun and the moon!

"Oh, Papa!"

I wanted to throw my arms around him and say, "Papa, I love you!" But I couldn't. Out of the need to numb myself against my feelings of pain and anger, I had numbed myself against all feelings. I especially couldn't express warmth. I just stood there, beaming, "Papa, I...."

"I know," smiled my father.

He and I went down to register at McGill the very next morning without telling my mother who, despite the fact that my father was doing so well now, would be sure to object.

When we came back home together at noon, she was waiting for us in the kitchen and glowering.

She looked from my father to me and back again with narrowed eyes. "Where did you two go this morning?" Her voice was that of the Grand Inquisitor.

My father made his escape. He hated scenes and confrontations.

I decided to face her. But I handled it poorly.

"He registered me at McGill." My voice wobbled.

"What? You're going to go to day school? Like a parasite?"

"Yes." I wanted to say, "Look, Pa is doing so well now. We moved to this beautiful apartment. You have a fur coat. Mitch will certainly be going to McGill if he gets in. I've been working since I was fourteen. Why shouldn't I benefit too?" But I could say none of those things.

"Ma," my voice came out unsure. "With the credits I've accumulated at Sir George, I can graduate in just two years."

I walked into my bedroom, sat down at my desk and began to look over my mouth-watering schedule for the year. I still had a long list of books to buy.

My mother had followed me and now appeared in my doorway.

"Parasite!" she hissed. "Parasite!"

My stomach cramped. A sharp pain shot through my temple.

* * * *

I made few friends at McGill. But I flourished academically and got straight A's. At Sir George, I had been majoring in English. Here, I became interested in Psychology and Sociology which I felt were more real than an ivory tower subject like English since they were involved with people. Whole new worlds opened up to me!

A very popular course and also my favorite, was "The Sociology of the Family," which required a 30 page term paper. Since my father talked incessantly about his side of the family, I had a great deal to say and wrote 55 pages. The course grades were largely based on this paper, and, because the class was so large, covered an entire wall at the end of the term.

With my inferiority complex, I typically began searching for my name at the bottom of the list. When I had gone half way through the three hundred names and still had not found myself, hot tears started in my eyes. I had failed!

Just then, someone came running over to me.

"Sylvia, where are you looking? You came first!"

Part 3

A Search for Help

Chapter 7

New York - 1961

My Assembly-line Mexican divorce had left me feeling utterly dehumanized. Bereft.

Everything churned inside me as I left Juarez early that Saturday morning. I just had to talk to someone. My brother!

The bus from Newark Airport let me off in Greenwich Village. My brother lived only a few blocks away. Since it was not yet one o'clock, I knew he'd be home. I called and asked if I could come over. He said, "Sure."

Ten minutes later, I rang the bell of his West Thirteenth Street apartment.

The minute I saw him at his door looking tall, handsome, and self-possessed in his boxer shorts and hairy chest, I knew I shouldn't have come.

Mitch opened his arms to hug me. "Poor old Sylvia."

I cringed.

He stood back. "Here. Let's have a look at you!"

He looked so much like my father, I was startled. The same light hair, broad brow, ruddy cheeks, straight nose that ended in a little square tip. Only the eyes were different. The eyes were cold. Now those porcelain eyes appraised me.

I became aware of my rumpled linen coat, my limp hair that hadn't been washed in a week.

His stare zeroed in on the half-belted coat whose hem was coming down.

"We-e-ll, ye-e-es," he drawled. "Why must you always look like something the cat dragged in, Syl? No wonder you couldn't hold him!"

My brother had learned his lesson well from my mother.

My lips moved, but I couldn't seem to say anything.

"Come, sit down!" He motioned to his grey couch.

I sat down on the edge of the seat, legs crossed, clutching my pocketbook on my lap as though I were afraid he'd steal it. He sat down opposite me.

Would we ever get to talk about my divorce?

He smiled his false smile showing too many teeth. "So!"

I took a deep breath, "Mitch -"

He interrupted me. "Well, what do you think of it?"

"What?" What on earth was he talking about?

"My mustache, of course."

"What? Oh, it's - it's - Listen, Mitch, I've been through such -"

"You like it?"

"Yes, it's fine. Mitch, listen -"

"Does it do anything for me?"

I stared at him. How could anyone be so callous? But I had never been able to communicate with Mitch. He had always used words not to share emotions and ideas but to obscure whatever it was he was thinking.

I met his eye.

"Look, Mitch, maybe it was a mistake to come."

"Well..." That smile again. "I am expecting a call. And I have a date later."

"You want me to go?"

"You probably want some lunch first?" He led me to his kitchenette and opened the refrigerator door. "Let's see what we have here. A half can of tuna. Whew! Can't stand how it smells." He threw it into the garbage. "And some cheese. I wouldn't recommend that either. A half bottle of Chianti and....Say, you want a beer?"

He had known me all his life and didn't know that I didn't drink beer.

"Look, Mitch, I'm not really interested in food. When is your date?"

He paused. "Around five."

"Would it be all right if I took a half hour nap? It's only one thirty. Then, I'll leave, and you can go about your business."

"Suits me. I'll go into my bedroom and leave the door ajar."

I lay down on the couch, tension cramping my whole body. I put my head on a pillow and tried hard to empty my mind and relax. My glance strayed to the graceful curve of the scimitar on my brother's wall. Its sharp blade looked threatening to say the least, and I wondered why Mitch would choose to decorate his apartment in such an unusual fashion.

Then, I remembered the story behind the scimitar. I had heard it years ago.

For some months, he had rented his bedroom to an Arab student who had become a great friend. In arrears in his rent and short of funds, the Arab, before leaving the U.S., had offered Mitch this curved saber with its hand carved ivory handle in payment, but also as a bond of friendship.

Mitch had delighted in telling this story to my parents, knowing that they would see in the Arab friend and his saber a symbol of Mitch's total rejection of their Jewish values.

Gradually, I dozed off. I must have fallen into a sound sleep for I was startled to be awakened by the phone in the next room. My brother's voice, oozing charm, drifted in.

"Hiya, Marty! Good to hear from you! I hear that......" He guffawed. "Hey, that's rich! Well, thank you. Thank you very much. Guess I'm just lucky!"

So Mitch had gotten another raise or promotion. He had the boundless confidence of one who knows beyond a shadow of a doubt he's loved by his mother. And his bosses on Madison Avenue appreciated that.

"No, Marty. No. I'd love to but I can't. It's not that I don't have the time. No. You see, unfortunately, my sister's here. No! Believe me, you wouldn't want to meet her. Oh, I don't know. She's a sad sack. Well, you know, she just got divorced. Yeah. Yeah. Maybe what she needs is a good lay." He chuckled.

I grabbed my pocketbook and suitcase, stumbled out of the apartment, and slammed the door behind me.

* * * *

"Honestly, Dr. Westron, it was so devastating! It was like I failed at the most important thing I ever tried. I never want to relive those few days of my life if I live to be...."

"Just a minute!" My therapist, Dr. Westron, had picked up the phone in her fineboned hand. A gold filigreed bracelet gleamed on her wrist.

"Western Union? I want to send a telegram to Dr. Arnold Hauser. That's H-a-u-s-e-r at 379 East 79th Street, New York." She crossed her shapely legs and patted the sleek, auburn coil on her finely sculpted head. "Yes. No. Not 'o-u'. I said 'a-u'. That's right. I want it to read, 'Happy Fortieth. Lots of love'. And sign it with my name. 'Ann'. That's right. And bill it to me." She gave her name and address. "Thank you."

She hung up the phone, her smile fading. "Yes, Sylvia, you were saying?"

I was so enraged at her interrupting me that I sat quivering.

"Well," I didn't know what to do. Should I tell her how much she had upset me by interrupting me just then? But I didn't know how to show anger. I had never learned how. All my life had been spent restraining my anger at my mother. I also didn't know how to assert myself. I never had. Anywhere.

I decided not to mention how I felt. "Dr. Westron I'm...I've been so devastated since I got back from Mexico, so defeated. And then that ghastly, awful reception by my brother..." I began to sob. "I don't know where to turn. How to get through the days."

"Just a minute." Dr. Westron picked up the phone again. "Western Union? This is Dr. Westron again. I just sent a telegram to Dr. Arnold Hauser. That's H-A-U-S-E-R. Just five minutes ago. That's right. I want to change the wording of that. I said before, 'Happy Fortieth. Lots of love.' I'd like you to change that to 'Happy fortieth. You're not getting older. You're getting better. All my love.' Please read that back to me. Fine. What are the charges on that? Thank you." She hung up.

"You were saying?"

By now, I was boiling. "Dr. Westron, here I was in the middle of telling you something I find so excruciating ab..about my divorce. And you interrupted me. You interrupted me twice, breaking into my thoughts. It's so..." I lost courage, and my voice trailed away.

"Sylvia, I'm sure it's no news to you that you're a very hostile person."

"Oh, I see. The customer's always wrong!"

"See what I mean?"

I clenched my teeth.

"That's why you always found fault with your mother. She did this to you. She did that to you. You talk about your mother being hostile. It's you who's hostile. That's why you could never get along with her. That's why you couldn't get along with your husband. Or your brother. And you're showing exactly the same behavior here. Typical."

I felt I was sitting on barbed wire.

"But...."

"You've heard the term 'transference'? You know what it means?"

"That you transfer emotions from one relationship to another," I whispered.

"Can't you see what you're doing?"

"What?"

"Transferring your anger from your mother to me. And your competitiveness. Have you any idea how much you compete with her?"

A shiver rippled through me.

"You've talked about your husband, Henry, having such a temper. How do you know it wasn't your hostility that made him angry?"

I began to sputter.

"But he...but he...I was always exhausted at the end of a long day of teaching. Yet, if I didn't have his soup waiting for him on the table the moment he walked in the door, he'd get furious and throw things. And once...once...he...once, when he didn't have the car, and he picked me up after work, I dared sit down on the subway on the way home, and he...he...yelled.....he s-s-screamed at me."

Dr. Westron looked skeptical. "What did he say?"

I choked out the words with great difficulty.

"That - that he was a-ashamed to have a wife who was such a weakling she....she had to sit down on the subway! Now, of course, I knew...knew that he was a Holocaust survivor and had learned the hard way that you must never show weakness. That if you do they come and get you. So - I understood. So screaming at me made him feel better. But what about my needs? I was exhausted. I needed to sit down. I was also tense. I needed someone to talk to. He was never there for me."

Dr. Westron sighed.

"Sylvia, I've never seen anyone so good at avoiding essentials. You told me he only wanted to have sex when he was in the mood. Never when you were."

"That's right. He was not at all sensitive to me. He never...."

"That's the crux of it. Why do you think a man should dominate in that area?"

I thought for a moment. "Oh, I understand what you're saying. But shouldn't he...?"

"That's the whole problem. And it's *your* problem that *you* have to face. You refused to accept his *domination*."

I felt I was going crazy. Henry had never tried to please me. In nearly five years of marriage, we had never seen a movie of my choice. Or had friends of my choosing visit. Once or twice when we did, Henry was so rude they never called again. I knew something was wrong with Dr. Westron's reasoning. But I couldn't think clearly enough to figure out what it was. Or could she be right? *Should* I have accepted his domination?

"Dr. Westron, I feel so splintered....so confused. I don't know what's right or wrong any more. Since my divorce, I've been in so many pieces - like a broken mirror. I thought I wanted this divorce. But now I'm petrified. Suppose I never meet anyone again who...."

I began to sob again. "...who will want me....Dr. Westron, I feel as if I'm about to have a nervous breakdown."

Dr. Westron lit a long cigarette from a silver cigarette case and crossed her shapely legs again. "Please! Please don't have it in this office." Her eyes swept across her oriental rug as though she was afraid I'd desecrate it. "I have my reputation to consider."

I left Dr. Westron's office and walked mindlessly west on Eighty-eighth Street.

I had messed up my life. I was flawed. Had a crack running through me.

I crossed Madison Avenue where I narrowly missed being hit by a car.

"Why don't you look where you're going?" the driver hollered.

I kept walking against the light with cars honking at me from all directions. The blare of the horns and the sharp grating of brakes from busses, trucks, and taxis bewildered me.

In Central Park, I sat down on a bench next to an old black woman with a weatherbeaten face under an orange turban, nursing all her worldly possessions in a shopping cart.

It began to rain.

I must have looked utterly forlorn sitting there in the rain, for the woman, smelling of sweat, urine, and beer, slid over to me. Her voice was soft and warm. "You don't have no home to go to, honey?"

I was flooded with emotions that jostled inside me. Terror that this bag lady identified me with herself. What did that say about me? Terror about the future. Would I, too, be alone and friendless and homeless some day when I was old? At the same time, I was overwhelmed with compassion for her and more than touched by her kindness.

As these feelings warred in me, I had, apparently, been staring into space, for she moved still closer to me and touched my bare upper arm with a calloused hand. I cringed. Then I hated myself.

"You don't have no home to go to, honey? Don't be ashamed. You can tell me."

I turned my head slightly toward her. My slanting glance showed me how few teeth she had. I fumbled inside my pocketbook, pulled out some crumpled bills, tossed them at her, and fled.

Now that I had left Henry, did I have a home?

When I had bravely come to New York, partly to get away from my mother, my father decided to follow me here, and my mother had no choice but to join him against her wishes. My father had been able to do the almost impossible. In his late fifties, with very little help from anyone, he had been able to conquer the New York real estate market and make contact with such real estate tycoons as Lefrak, Tishman, Trump. He had done very well.

So, if I wished, I could go "home" to my parents, two lonely people who didn't talk to each other, who now owned a handsome house and garden in Manhattan Beach in Brooklyn. My mother glowered at my father and at me and didn't leave us alone together for an instant. In addition, I dreaded facing my father's commiseration and my mother's I-told-you-so derision. After all, hadn't she told me since I was six that no man would stay with me if I didn't mend my ways?

I had been living in New York twelve years now, and what had I accomplished? Precious little. I had acquired a Master's in Education. Since there had been few positions for High School English teachers, and, since I was terrified of teenagers anyway, my bright sixth graders were being treated to an unusual curriculum. They wrote their own plays out of research they themselves did to supplement the dry Social Studies text. We created our own poetry journal. Each child wrote his own autobiography that he illustrated with a self-portrait. I was "reaching" the children, and it was immensely gratifying.

But even here I was having problems. My principal was most disapproving. My desks weren't straight. Nor were the window blinds even. He had found a tiny piece of paper behind the door. And once, when I was in the throes of depression about my divorce, he had caught me committing the most heinous crime of all. Sitting down. Perhaps Henry had told him about me! Later, a nasty note found its way into my permanent file.

Everything else in my life had crumbled.

Dr. Westron was not my first therapist since I had come here. She was the third. My last therapist had been Dr. Leonard, a charming Viennese who had been most sympathetic to me.

He had kept clucking as I talked on and on about Henry.

"Look, I have an idea," he had said after about a year. "German Jews are very different from Russian Jews like yourself. From you description, Henry sounds very Prussian."

"Oh, he certainly is!"

"Would you say Henry is like his father?"

"Oh, very much so. His father also has the Prussian idea that his wife was put on earth to serve him and that his soup must be on the table the moment he steps in the door."

"And how does Henry's mother get along with him?"

I thought a moment. "Pretty well, I think. We visit them often, and I've never heard them quarrel."

Dr. Leonard smiled. "Then, there's your answer. Why don't you watch carefully to see how Henry's mother manages his father. Then, all you have to do is follow suit."

I watched. What I saw was that Henry's father would ask his mother to lie down on a bed of nails if the fancy struck him. And that his mother would do it.

Suddenly, something crystallized in me. I was *not* going to live like that. I would divorce Henry.

When I phoned Henry's mother, Katie, to say good-bye to her, she, at first, tried hard to dissuade me.

"Oh, Sylvia, I was so afraid it would come to this. I've always loved you like a daughter. And I've never understood Henry and his rages. Just like his father. But maybe you should try to bend a little more. That's what we women have to do, you know. Bend. Submit. After all, you teach children. But Henry teaches at a university. He may be under more strain. And, after all, you know what he's been through...."

"I know, Katie. I'm always making allowances."

"Sylvia, try to be more patient. Maybe if you had a baby. Yes! That's the answer! A baby would warm him up. Babies are what hold marriages together. I always say, 'You live with your husband but you love your children.'"

"Katie, I'm happy you want to keep me. But I don't think a baby is the answer." I was terrified of having a baby. Especially with someone like Henry. I could just imagine the kind of father he'd make.

"Sylvia, don't be hasty. Please think it over carefully. That's all I ask." Suddenly, she burst into tears. "Oh, Sylvia, if I had a profession like you, if I could make a living for myself, as you do, do you think I would have wasted my whole life on Leo?"

And this was the woman I was supposed to emulate!

What she said corroborated my decision to get the divorce. It also made me realize that Dr. Leonard, whom I liked so much personally, had not been helpful at all. In giving me the well-meaning advice he did, he was not taking my needs into account.

The therapist I had seen prior to Dr. Leonard had been worse. He had been a strict Freudian who, in the year I had spent my entire salary on him, had not said a single word except "Hmm." Once when I looked up, I found him asleep.

After Dr. Westron, who had felt my basic problem was my hostility to my mother which I was transferring to her and my refusal to accept Henry's domination, I saw yet another therapist. Therapist number four, also highly recommended.

Like Dr. Westron, Dr. Rodney had his own idea of what my problem was.

Around this time, I read a fable about a Greek innkeeper, Procrustus, who had only one bed. When a customer was too short, he stretched him to fit the bed. When he was too tall, he cut his legs off. I often thought that all these therapists, but especially Dr. Rodney, were like Procrustus.

They were ingenious at twisting each patient like a pretzel to fit their pet theory.

Dr. Rodney's theory was that I had a severe Oedipus, or

rather, Electra complex. I was far too intensely attached to my father to be able to relate to any man and, moreover, was competing with my mother for his love which was the reason for all the friction between us. Pure and Simple. Elementary.

"Look, Dr. Rodney, I'm sure there's some element of that in it always. But I don't feel that's the answer. It just doesn't strike a chord."

Dr. Rodney sat very still, his round moon face smiling.

"Are you implying I couldn't love Henry because I'm too attached to my father? That that's why the marriage broke up?"

"Now we're getting somewhere."

"Look, Dr. Rodney, I love my father. I don't think I'd have survived without him. But I'm not attached to him in that way. Honest. I wasn't even jealous when he had Edith. I was happy for him. And when my parents came to New York, I could have lived with them. But I was so eager not to, I always sought a job at the far end of another borough so I couldn't possibly. In fact, I've seen very little of him since we've been in New York because I thought it was very good for me to break away....."

"You're going to have to stop resisting, Sylvia."

"What do you mean?"

"What do you think I mean? You're going to have to face your feelings about your father and stop whitewashing them. You have to recognize your feelings and acknowledge them. Otherwise, your relationships with men will never improve."

"But....."

"You're still resisting."

"Look. Can we talk about something else?"

"Sure. All right. Let's talk about some other relationships you've had with men and see if we can find a pattern. Whom did you date before Henry?"

"Someone I met at Columbia Graduate School, called George Finkle."

"Tell me what happened with George."

"I saw him for over a year. I enjoyed his sense of humor."

"Yes?"

"He wanted me to go to bed with him."

"And?" That smile again.

"Well, naturally, I didn't."

"Aha! Because you were too attached to your father!"

"No. Because I was petrified of sex. You don't know how I was raised by my mother. Montreal was the most Puritanical society in the world. And my mother kept dinning it into me that no man would respect me if I let him touch me. When I came to New York, I had to work on myself for years till I was even able to neck. George was really the first man I necked with. I was crazy about him. But I wasn't ready to go to bed with him. I wasn't ready to go to bed with anyone till I was married. I had to be married."

"And what happened with George?"

"One night, as the subway came hurtling down a tunnel, George asked me to marry him. Can you see this picture? There was all this ear-splitting screeching and rattling of the subway and a hundred perspiring people crowding around us. I was sitting. George was standing over me. Suddenly, I thought I heard him yell, 'Will you marry me?' I shouted, 'What?' He shouted back, 'I said, 'Will you marry me?'' It was so funny yet so sad. It could have been such a beautiful moment in both our lives. But he had made it so ugly and demeaning. Why do you think he proposed that way?"

He shrugged. "Maybe he was afraid you'd hear him."

I laughed sourly. "That's how I felt. That he didn't love me. That he wanted me to say 'No'."

"What happened?"

"I was so hurt at this so-called proposal, I felt like...like a...worm. But I didn't know how to tell him that. And what good would it have done? Besides, I felt vaguely that it was, somehow, my fault. No. I didn't feel that vaguely. I really felt that."

"What did you feel?"

"That it was my fault. He couldn't love me because I was somehow unlovable. It was such an awful feeling."

I was eager to probe this feeling that I was unlovable. I now had a hunch it lay at the core of so many of my problems. But he interrupted me.

"What happened then?"

"I had hoped he'd perhaps call to tell me he loved me. But he didn't call me at all. Two weeks later, I learned from a mutual friend that he had married someone else! Can you imagine! To him girls were interchangeable!" I took a deep, wavering breath. "It was devastating!" I sighed. "Six months later, I met Henry."

Dr. Rodney made no response to my story. He kept prodding me to recognize the underlying sexual feelings I had for my father.

But, by the time I left for Israel fourteen months later, I still had made no progress.

On one level, I saw it as yet another failure on my part. On the other, I was frustrated that after hundreds of hours (I saw Dr. Rodney three times a week) and thousands upon thousands of words, I had not succeeded in breaking down the wall between us. Dr. Rodney's concept of me had not changed in the slightest. And, in my heart, I knew he was wrong. Should I just mouth the words he wished me to mouth in the hope that, eventually, I would get to believe them?

I thought not.

Chapter 8

Before I left for Israel, I knew I had to say good-bye to my Aunt Sarah, my father's sister.

Sarah lived in a shtetl-like enclave of four related families who had all settled within a three block radius of the Grand Concourse and 174th Street in the West Bronx. The richest of these families, that of her cousin Manya, daughter of her mother's sister, had a penthouse on the roof of an elegant apartment building on the Concourse itself. Sarah, the poorest, lived on Morris Avenue in a fourth floor walkup.

I rang her bell. The door was opened by Aunt Sarah, a short, fat woman with a bun on top of her head in the shape of a challah. She wore dime store earrings that dangled down to her shoulders. Sarah had lived in New York since 1911, more than fifty years. Yet, she always managed to look and sound as if she just came off the boat. Her ancient discolored satin blouse was cracked along the seams. On her feet, she wore the same worn corduroy men's slippers, inside the house and out, summer and winter. Shoes were too expensive. Her huge bosom cascaded over her flimsy dime store brassiere. "Real brassieres were too expensive," said Sarah.

Sarah was married to Itsie, an egg candler who talked only about eggs - how much it hurts a chicken to lay an egg, how many eggs a chicken lays a day, a week, a month, how often you find double yolks, and so forth. Having worked for ten years in a sweat shop and having married Itsie for the express purpose of escaping the sweat shop, Sarah's object in life was to subsist on Itsie's meager earnings which never rose to more than fifty dollars a week. This she did by living on the cracked eggs Itsie brought home for free. Her eyes blinked incessantly behind the thick glasses.

"Sylvia," she scolded me. "Again you come bringing a Times. Think what my neighbors will say! That my niece is a snob! Why can't you read the Daily News like everybody else?"

I strongly suspected that when Sarah first came to the sweat

shop she may have boasted that she came from a wealthy home and
had the starch knocked out of her because of it. She had thus
learned that you must never, never show you are better than anyone
else.

I kissed her. "How have you been Sarah? You feeling okay?"

"So far, thank God. How's your father?"

"It was only a mild stroke, the doctor said. They say he'll get
over it. But he's taking longer to recover than I thought. It's so
painful to see him that way, Sarah."

"He's so young for a stroke. Not yet seventy. It's very far,
but I'd visit him in a minute if it weren't for your mother. She treats
me like...."

Sarah and I both knew that my parents had moved out to
Manhattan Beach for two reasons. First, my father wanted to buy a
house, and he adored the ocean. And, secondly, my mother couldn't
abide her husband's family.

"She's such a big shot," Sarah said bitterly "She doesn't know
what I know about her."

"What do you mean?"

"Never mind."

What did Sarah know? But I had other things on my mind
today.

"I came to say good-bye, Sarah. I'm leaving for Israel. I've
been talking about it for years. I've been eager to meet my mother's
family, and, now that I'm divorced, it's the perfect time."

"You're going when your father is sick?"

"That's what I wanted to discuss with you. First of all, I'm
only going for the summer. I hoped he'd be better by now. He is.
Only not as much as I hoped. But I'm so depressed. I need a
change. I simply must get away from everything. Can you understand that, Sarah?"

Her eyes blinked more rapidly.

"As a matter of fact, I do understand. Remember, I was once
divorced myself. I still remember the lummox my father arranged for
me to marry. A mean bastard with an ugly face and no hair. Itsie

isn't much, believe me. But at least he has a head full of black curls. Or rather he did when I married him. How was I to know that soon he'd be as bald as one of his eggs? Where was I? Oh, yes. Why I came to America. I felt I just had to get away from everything, too. So I understand how you feel." She sighed. "If only your father was better."

"Sarah, you don't think I'm an awful person for leaving?"

"I don't know." She blinked at me for a long moment. "You know what, Sylvia? Go. Go! The young are more important than the old. It'll do you good. I think your father would want you to go."

"Gee, thanks, Sarah. I'm glad you feel that way. Now I don't feel so guilty for leaving. Sarah, listen, I was going to take you and Itsie out on your fortieth anniversary. But I'm leaving in a few days, and there won't be time. So I'm giving you these tickets for ANNIE GET YOUR GUN."

Sarah's eyes popped.

"What? What did you say? Tickets? What kind of tickets?"

It was as I suspected. She had never been to a Broadway show.

"For ANNIE GET YOUR GUN. It's a play. A musical show. On Broadway. Or, rather, it's on West 46th Street just west of Broadway."

"Sylvia," she sighed "why do you talk so funny, like a Canadian. You're not supposed to say 'Broadway'. You say 'Br-r-roadvay.'" She rolled her "r" roundly and placed the accent on the "vay".

I suppressed a smile. Poor Sarah. "I'll remember," I told her. "Now about the tickets. They're for next Saturday afternoon."

Sarah stood looking down at her slippers. "Yes, the tickets."

"What's the matter, Sarah?"

She flushed from her neckline for her forehead. "I...don't think we can use them."

"Why not?"

Her eyes filled with tears, and she cracked her knuckles.

"Itsie won't want to spend the carfare."

"What carfare?"

"On the subway. It's fifteen cents for each of us each way." She flushed more deeply. "That's sixty cents."

I pressed a dollar into her hands.

Her jaw dropped. "Finally - so I'm, finally, going - to see a play on Broadway. Fifty years in New York, and I'm finally....finally...going to see a play. Finally..." Tears rained down her cheeks.

* * * *

"Hi, Pa. How are you?" I propped up his pillow on his chair and turned it toward the window so he could look into his garden and the ocean beyond it.

He mumbled something. His jaw seemed loose. But he did not otherwise look as if he'd had a stroke.

"You feel okay, Pa?" I kissed his forehead.

He mumbled again.

"Where's Ma?"

"Ma?"

"Yes. Where's Ma?"

He collected himself. "Shopping. She went shopping."

"Good. Then, we can talk alone. How do you feel?"

He stared blankly at the cherry tree outside the window. Then he seemed to wake up. "Zviahleh, it's you? It's really you?" He took my hand and squeezed it.

"It's me. I came to see you." I kissed him again.

"It's really you?"

"It's me."

"You came all the way to Montreal to see me?"

"No. We all live in New York now, Pa."

"I'm in New York?"

"That's right."

He stared at the cherry tree and the ocean. "That's New York?"

"Yes. You live near the ocean. You love the ocean."

He shook his head, puzzled. "What happened to me?"

"You had a tiny stroke. They say it's nothing, and you'll soon get over it. You're better each time I see you. Pa, I came to say good-bye. I'm going to Israel for the summer. By the time I get back in the fall, you'll be all better, and I'll tell you about Israel."

"What? Zviahleh, what did you say?"

I said slowly. "I said I'm going to Israel, Pa."

"To Israel?"

"That's right."

"So you're going to Israel. And when are you leaving?"

"On Tuesday."

"Uhu. So you're leaving on Tuesday. And when will you be back?"

"I'll be back in the fall. I'm only going for the summer."

"I see. So you're going for the summer. And you're going to Israel."

"Right."

"And when did you say you're leaving?"

"On Tuesday."

"Oh, so you're leaving on Tuesday."

"That's right."

"I see. And how long will you be gone?"

Round and round.

I tried to break through this fog. It was like pushing through cobwebs.

"Pa, listen to me. Pa...."

"Wha....."

"Pa, there's something I need to tell you."

"What?"

"Pa, listen. Pa, are you listening?"

With a visible effort he looked up and met my eyes.

"Oy, Zviahleh, it's so good to see you," he beamed.

"Pa, there's something I want to explain. Pa, I've been so depressed since my break up with Henry. I feel so ...empty. I felt miserable enough during the marriage. I feel worse now."

"I know, Ketzeleh. It breaks my heart. I had a strong feeling from the start that he was not for you, but what could I do? You - seemed so..." he groped for the word, "sure."

"I wasn't sure, Pa," I whispered. "I was desperate. He was bright and ambitious, and he asked me. I didn't think anyone else ever would."

My father squeezed out a small smile. "Zviahleh, why do you...why do you..."

"Pa, I still didn't explain why I'm leaving now. Pa, I just can't face the long summer. I'll be all alone. Not working. Not being busy. Not being with people. I can't bear it. That's why I decided to go to Israel. It'll be a change. I'll meet Ma's family. It will help me forget. On the other hand, I feel so guilty leaving you now that you're sick. Pa, what do you think?"

My father stared at the floor for a long moment. Then he looked up at me, his eyes misty. "Zviahleh," he emphasized each separate word, "I've - lived my - life -. It's - your - turn -now."

"Papa! Oh, Papa, you're so wonderful!" I hugged him. "I know I'll feel a lot better in the fall. So will you. The doctor said so."

There was a long pause.

"Zviahleh," he took a deep breath and grasped my hands. "If you want to do something for me."

"Anything, Pa."

"You know what I'm going to ask."

"What?"

"Make up with Ma."

His words fell with a dull plop.

"Pa!" I felt a humming in my ears. How could he ask me that? As if it were in my power to change the relationship! As if I was the cause of the hostility between us! "Pa, what are you talking about?"

"It kills me the way you hardly talk to her."

I pulled my hands away. Anger surged through me. Didn't he empathize with me at all for all the pain she had caused me all my life? How dare he ask this of me? How unfair of him to tell me how badly I was making him feel! Why didn't he stand up for me more often? Didn't he ever feel guilty that he had given me the mother he had? I was strangling.

"You don't know what you're asking, Pa. How you're making me feel!"

"Zviahleh, now that I'm sick, she's so alone."

"She's not alone. She has her darling Mitch!" The words shot out sharper than I intended.

"What are you talking about, Zviahleh? She doesn't have Mitch! Since he left for California a year ago, how many times has he called her. Two? Three? You know Mitch. Mitch is - He's -" my father looked drained.

"Does she ever get mad at him?" I asked bitterly.

"No," he heaved a sigh. "She makes excuses for him."

"I know. In his entire life, he's never done anything wrong."

"Zviahleh," he seemed to have run out of strength, "Please, Zviahleh," he whispered. "You're all your mother has. She needs you. She loves you...." His words were barely audible.

What he was asking seemed so unjust, I was dumbfounded. But there was, apparently, no way I could make him understand. And he was ill. I didn't want to upset him. And what did he mean she loved me? And why was it so much easier for me to get angry with him than with her?"

I felt I was being torn to shreds.

"Pa, would you like a nice cup of tea?" I asked brightly, busying myself in the kitchen. "I'll make it for you the Russian way in a tall glass with a lump of sugar."

Doing something practical was a wonderful way to avoid thinking and facing problems and finding solutions.

My father began to sip the tea through the large square lump of sugar he held between his teeth. Then, with the glass still in his hand, he dozed off. His jaw dropped, and he began to snore.

I took the glass out of his hand, then sat and watched him sleep. I longed to stay with my father till my mother returned so he need not be alone. On the other hand, I was tempted to leave so I need not see her. After he had slept fifteen minutes, I decided to leave.

But as I reached the door, I heard my mother's key in the lock and came face to face with her.

"What?" she exploded as she saw me. "You were going to leave without even seeing me?"

"Ma, we don't get along."

That was putting it mildly.

"And you sneaked in to see your father when I wasn't home? So you could be alone with him."

My stomach cramped.

"Ma, I came to say good-bye to him. I'm leaving for Israel on Tuesday. I told you a dozen times. Is it okay if I say good-bye to my own father who's sick before I go?"

"Just look at that! You're going to Israel, and I'll never be able to go! Can you imagine how that makes me feel? How that burns me up?"

"Ma, you can go if you wish."

"How can I go with your father sick? Are you crazy?"

"Ma, I'm going to give everyone your regards. And I'll faithfully report back to you about your whole family. Now I have to go."

Part 4

Interlude in Israel

Chapter 9

Norman and I were lying in a sexual tangle in my bed in my Brooklyn Heights apartment. We had both dozed off afterwards. Now I had awakened.

I gazed at him sleeping so contentedly in the Saturday morning sunshine and smiled.

I hadn't known sex could be so delicious.

During our marriage, Henry had been so bumbling and inept, and I had been so raw and green that I hadn't even dreamt of its possibilities.

The secret lay in knowing how.

Norman knew how.

Everything about my romance with Norman seemed enchanted, starting with how we met. For we had met in Israel.

* * * *

Going to Israel when I did was, I had to admit, a stroke of genius. For a long time, I had been eager to meet my mother's illustrious family. Now the timing was perfect. The excitement, I hoped, would pull me out of my post-divorce doldrums. I went, planning to stay just the summer, but, when I learned my father was better, I stayed a whole year. My father encouraged me.

My mother's family consisted of many fascinating personalities, and I reveled in the attention and love and warmth they showered on me. I was more than grateful that all these aunts and uncles, even my Uncle Dovid who had lived up to his promise and become a well-known writer, translator, and literary critic, appeared to accept me. But soon I realized that, while they loved me, they did not love me for myself. Their English and my Hebrew were both too poor for true communication. And none of them were taking the time. They loved me as the daughter of their long lost sister, Dvorah, who had been so brutally snatched from them and carried off by that ogre - my father.

They had sanctified my mother.

"Such a wonderful girl."

"So cheerful and gay. Always singing."

"A heart of gold."

"She nursed all of us when we were sick."

"And beautiful. She could have married anyone."

"So many men were after her. I envied her so much."

"That she should throw herself away on -."

They could hardly bear to mention my father's name.

"What kind of father was he?" they asked. I could see from their faces that had I told them he fried me in boiling oil once a week they would not have been surprised. I dreaded offending them. But I did want to set the record straight.

"A very loving father," I whispered, carefully not saying the kind of mother she was. They glared at me and exchanged glances. The subject never came up again.

"But, from what your mother writes, they get along quite well otherwise?" Layah, the feisty one, pried, watching my face closely.

"Yes," I smiled and changed the subject. My mother's secret would be safe with me.

I often thought of what I had lost - how different my childhood and my whole life would have been had I been raised in Palestine surrounded by this huge, warm family who would have compensated for my mother's coldness to me. But no. Had we lived in Palestine, she would not have been the same kind of mother! And my father, who would have been unhappy in Palestine, would have been a very different kind of husband and father! When you began to play the "what if" game, life certainly became very strange.

Socially, my life took on a golden glow in Israel.

I had learned some Hebrew from my mother in my childhood, but it was an old-fashioned Biblical Hebrew. Since I was so eager to date, I now learned quickly to speak colloquial Hebrew, through sheer motivation, and, of course, the help of my family.

And, to my astonishment, I was very popular.

I felt differently about myself in Israel. In Canada and the

United States, I had been a short, thin Jewess. In Israel, where the average person was considerably shorter, I became transformed into a tall, slender Anglo-Saxon. I had become a butterfly. I thoroughly enjoyed this metamorphosis.

I had been lonely for all of my thirty-four years. Now, three and four men a day were picking me up! One began to speak to me on a bus. He followed me home, and, by the time we reached my aunt Rivka's, had confessed how fond he was of me. On our first date, he proposed to me! It was eerie!

Another man, a very attractive one, proposed to me while we were waiting at a busy intersection for a long light to change.

I chalked up thirteen proposals in my first five months in Israel!

At first, it was intoxicating! Having been a wallflower all my life, it was delightful to be sought after.

Then I panicked. There had to be a catch. These men could not be interested in me! They saw me as a stereotypical American. Not one of my suitors had made the effort to get to know me as a person before proposing!

I felt faceless. Invisible.

In fact, the problems in my relationships with these men were very similar to those I encountered with my family. There was no way they could get to know me quickly nor I them. The subtleties were all lost in the language difficulty.

For a short time, I was happy to be invisible.

If these Israeli men knew the real me, wouldn't they also reject me as the American men had? After all, even my own mother hadn't been able to love me. So maybe I was fortunate our communication was so poor.

No! I had stepped into water too deep for me.

Now I understood. All these men had spotted that I was an American. By my clothes or my shoes or the fact that I was reading Newsweek magazine on the bus. They were all after my American passport.

I discovered Israel consisted of two kinds of people. The

idealists, people like my relatives who felt privileged to be there and were doing everything in their power against almost insuperable odds to build up their country and those who had been forced to come to Israel against their wishes because they had nowhere else to go. These were always seeking opportunities to leave Israel. The easiest way was by marrying an American.

This was the ugly side of Israel that no one talked about. And it was frightening.

The last thing I needed was a second disastrous marriage with someone out to exploit me.

It was too dangerous to remain in Israel. Having been so lonely all my life, it would be too easy to be seduced into marrying one of these suitors and fall into a trap.

* * * *

Despite my fears about coping with teenagers, I had obtained a job as English teacher at a high school in Tel Aviv. It was the only job for which I was qualified. Having signed a contract, I decided to stay till the end of the school year in June and then leave.

It was in this discouraged frame of mind that I volunteered to supervise a dance at my school one Wednesday night in February. Since I was not dancing and had no one to talk to, the evening seemed endless.

Suddenly, a man walked in off the street. He was tall, muscular, handsome. He looked around the large gym and came directly over to me, the only adult in the room.

"I heard the music. I could never resist folk music."

He was speaking English!

"How did you know I spoke English?" I asked, flabbergasted.

"I knew." He smiled a long, slow smile. "Want to dance?"

We danced and didn't stop talking. It was so wonderful to be speaking English again! After two dances, he asked if he could take me home, and, forgetting all about my duties as supervisor, I left the dance to walk home with him.

It was winter. But an Israeli winter. On wet days it was raw, but on dry days it was delightful. This was a dry moonlit night. We walked home slowly to my hostel in North Tel Aviv, a walk of about an hour. On our way, we stopped for a chicken dinner at a restaurant near the tiny Yarkon River.

We never stopped talking. We had so much to say to each other! By the time we arrived at the Beit Borodetsky Hostel where I lived, I knew I was in love. We had so much in common, Norman and I. It was uncanny.

It turned out that, like me, he had been born in Odessa on the very street where my grandparents had lived. Bazarnya. And during the same month in 1927! Like my parents, his had also decided to leave the Soviet Union when he was an infant. And, like mine, they had also left for Istanbul. And, like my parents, his had also stayed till he was three years old!

There the parallels ended. His parents had emigrated to Palestine. They were poor and had settled in Jaffa. The Jewish population in Palestine was so small at that time that his mother was known to everyone as Hanna with the three sons. Norman, formerly Shlomo, was the middle one.

He talked about growing up under the British mandate where Jews were treated as "colonials" by the British. Norman had learned English in high school. But it was taught so poorly by people who knew so little English themselves that, when he graduated, he realized he knew only about a hundred words and was using them all wrong.

At this point, when he was about seventeen, he got a summer job in a radio repair shop. One day a red faced British major in a freshly pressed uniform strode in. He was so haughty, he actually wore a monocle and looked down with disdain at this little Jewish boy who was so eager to please him.

"Good morning, Sir," Norman smiled. "May I help you, Sir?"

The major put the radio he was carrying on the counter and glared at Norman. He had such a thick British accent, he sounded as if his mouth was full of oatmeal.

"I brought this radio in to be fixed last week." He stopped.

"Yes, Sir?" encouraged Norman.

"And you fucked it up!" He exploded. "You fucked up this fucking radio!"

"Yes, Sir!" Norman bowed from the waist, not having the slightest idea what the Major was talking about. "We'll take care of it, Sir."

The Major strode out, swinging his walking stick.

Norman was in a quandary. He had been able to get this job only because he had assured his boss he was really proficient in English. Particularly radio English. How could he now ask his boss what "fucked up" meant? To do so would reveal his ignorance. Besides, his boss knew even less English than he did. He began to search frantically in the radio manual in the shop. No "fuck". He found a much more complete manual and searched in that. Then he located the most comprehensive one of all. Still no "fuck"! He searched in several dictionaries. Nowhere could he find "fuck". He asked everyone he knew. They shrugged.

He tested the radio. True. It had a lot of static but when he took it apart, he could find nothing wrong with it.

He was now in a cold sweat. The Major was due to return for his radio the next day. He would lose his job. And he needed it so badly. Norman couldn't sleep all night. It was not till it occurred to him to look up a friend who had been in the British army that he, finally, found out what "fuck" meant!

By this time, we were both rocking with laughter.

Hand in hand, we walked out of the restaurant to the little wooden footbridge over the river and watched the willow trees on its banks dipping into the water.

Norman kissed me. "This has been the most wonderful evening of my life."

"Mine, too."

It turned out that Norman had gone to the United States to study engineering after the war, had obtained a good position at General Electric, and had settled in a suburb of Philadelphia. But after fourteen years in America, he had become homesick for his family in Israel so he had returned for a month. He was leaving the following Monday. But before he did, he planned to tour the country for a few days.

Would I join him?

Would I join him! I wanted to cry, "Yes! Yes! Yes!"

Then something began to trouble me. Norman was too old never to have married, particularly since he had no family in America. And since when did single people live in suburbs? Every fiber in me wanted to have an affair with him, but not if he were married. At the same time, I dreaded offending him with my suspicions.

Adopting my most jocular tone, I asked, "How do I know you're not married?"

He looked shocked. "Because I say so!"

I stood and stared at him.

"You don't believe me?"

"I want to believe you. Very much."

"Look, you want to leave it to fate?"

"What do you mean?"

"Well, I have a quarter here. Let's toss it. Heads we go away together. Tails we don't. Is that fair and square?"

"Okay," I laughed.

He tossed. It came out heads.

"Satisfied?" he grinned.

In a way, I was. Now I didn't feel guilty about breaking up a marriage, in the event he were married.

Visitors were not allowed to enter my hostel after nine o'clock so I could not invite Norman in. We arranged to meet the following day after work.

I ran upstairs to my apartment two steps at a time, my heart singing. This had been the best evening of my whole life! I had had a glorious time! I had not been self-conscious at all. Could that be because I was eight thousand miles away from my mother? Maybe it paid me to stay in Israel after all!

* * * *

That was the week-end I discovered sex.

Never had I felt so happy and so intensely alive. Norman's touch was magic. There was something wild about his lovemaking, yet he had exquisite control. I felt I was living in a dream, a moon trip from which I never wished to awaken.

Incidentally, we also did some sightseeing.

On the way back from Haifa on the sheroot, the communal taxi, Sunday night, his arm was around me as I lay against him all sleepy and cuddly. My fingers gently played with his shirt. Everyone politely averted their eyes as we kept kissing all the way back to Tel Aviv.

"I love you," he whispered. "Come back with me to America."

"I love you, too. But I can't leave. I have a contract."

"Break the contract."

"Darling, I can't."

He fingered my hair and did a feathery tracing on my neck.

"Break it."

"Norman," I kissed him. "Try to be reasonable. I'll come in June. The day school's over." I adored Norman, but I felt it would be foolish to follow him back to America on the strength of one single week-end. I wanted to test his love a little first. Besides, something told me it was wiser not to make it too easy for him.

He nuzzled in my bosom. "Can't wait that long."

"Why don't you stay here a few more days?"

"I can't. I have to get back to work."

"Even if I could leave now, how could I possibly get a teaching job in the United States at the end of February?"

"You'll find something."

"No, Norman. It's not a good idea."

"I love you so much."

"I love you too, dear. But I just can't come now."

"What's the earliest you can come?"

"Early June. The day school's over. But I'll be living in New York where I have a teaching license, not in Philadelphia."

He came up for air. "I'll come out every week-end."

He promised to write me the minute he got back home.

I floated through the next week, barely touching the ground. The whole world appeared bright around the edges as though everything wore a halo. I relived every delicious touch, every endearing phrase. I counted the weeks till we could be together again. Fifteen. The days. The hours. It all seemed too good to be true.

Turned out it was.

Exactly a week later, it arrived. The long airmail envelope.

It was very brief.

"Dearest Sylvia,

You are a wonderful girl with a delightful sense of humor and I love you as I've never loved anyone before. But our romance will have to end here.

All my love,
Norman"

I put down the letter, my hands shaking.

I wanted to scream. To throw things. How had this happened?

I ran next door to a girl from Chicago with whom I had become friendly.

"Pam, he's married! I was - I was seduced like - like a peasant!"

Pam did not look surprised. Wearing only a towel around her middle, she tossed her long honey hair over one thin shoulder and looked up from painting her toenails. "Men!"

"That's all you can say? 'Men!' Can you imagine how I feel? He was so smooth. He sounded so sincere. How do you know whom to believe? How could he lie like that? Through his teeth. And, like an idiot, I fell for it!"

"No wonder he was smooth. I bet he's had plenty of practice!"

Spots danced before my eyes. "Pam, he begged me to break

my contract and follow him to America."

Pam sighed. "Look, you wanted to have an affair, so you had an affair. Your mistake was to fall in love."

"What?"

"Listen. You want to get even with him?"

"Pam, what are you talking about?"

"Revenge is sweet. Too bad you don't have the guts. But if you did, I have a great plan. What you do is this.

"You have to steal some hotel stationery. Then you write a letter from the hotel to Mr. and Mrs. Norman What's-His-Name, thanking them for spending a week-end at your hotel and asking if everything was to their satisfaction. That should get his wife!"

"Pam, you're disgusting."

Pam smiled enigmatically and went back to her nails.

I returned to my room and studied the envelope again. It came not from Philadelphia, but from Paris! What was he doing in Paris when he had sworn he must be back at work immediately? He had lied about everything!

Then, I remembered something else. On our last day in Haifa, he had taken me into a gift shop and asked me to choose a really beautiful pendant for his "sister-in-law".

"Your sister-in-law?" I asked, surprised.

"Yes. I've been staying with my brother, and she's been very good to me. While you're at it, pick one out for yourself as well."

That seemed an odd way to give me a gift, I thought. I did pick one out for myself. But very reluctantly. Of course, the other pendant had been for his wife because at the moment, he had suffered a twinge of conscience. And he had had the gall to ask me to select it for him!

I felt sick to my stomach.

Now all the pieces of the jig-saw puzzle were falling in place. I had been stupid. As usual.

I was still happy I had had the week-end, but I knew now he had never loved me. He had used me! And laughed up his sleeve.

What a fool I'd been! I wanted to die of pain.

And it all only proved once more that I was unlovable.

* * * *

I desperately needed some to talk to.

Pam was so hard-boiled. At first, I thought of confiding in one of my aunts. Perhaps Rivka, who had been so sympathetic about my divorce. She was warm, and I liked her. But she was so old-fashioned. She had warned me that if I persisted in walking about the streets of Tel Aviv without a companion, I would get a bad reputation. How could I possibly confide in someone like that about an affair with a married man?

Instead, I drowned myself in my work, teaching English.

Chapter 10

My high school students had refined the term "chutzpah" to an art.

One boy kept correcting my English. "You're using the word 'keen' all wrong. See what it says in my dictionary?"

"I told you before, Shmuel, you can't learn English from a dictionary. Why are you wasting your time telling me I'm wrong? How will you ever learn English that way?"

"My father said the best way to get an A is to show you know more than the teacher!"

When I gave a test, another boy sat with his book open on his desk.

"Ari, you're cheating!"

"I'm not cheating. Cheating is when you do it secretly. I'm doing it openly!"

Their comments often made me reel.

Then, I made the monumental mistake of assigning a book review as a term paper.

On the day the reviews were due, I saw my mistake! Too late! I was deluged with beautifully written papers in flawless English.

They had all copied!

I knew that unless I could prove this conclusively to them by citing their original sources, I would completely lose credibility with them. But how to find the sources, and find them quickly enough? I spent the next few days in the American Library poring over every magazine I could find, searching for book reviews. After two days, I came up with one. My friend, Shmuel, had had the chutzpah to copy his review word from word from a two year old Life Magazine.

The following day, I stood a little taller at my desk with all the book reviews piled up in front of me.

I smiled and motioned to the papers on my desk.

"Your term papers were all written in such excellent English, it was a pleasure to read them."

They exchanged glances and smirked.

My tone remained honeyed. "I'm glad you learned so much from this class."

Their smiles grew broader.

Suddenly my voice grew hard. "I was just wondering, how come Shmuel's paper came directly from Life Magazine? Page 24. Can you explain that, Shmuel?"

Shmuel sat, his jaw hanging open. I heard several titters around the room.

My eyes narrowed. "I'll be happy to show anyone who doubts me the review in Life he copied from. Now," I fixed my eyes on them, "I'm going to throw out all those papers which are worthless." I heaped them in the waste paper basket. "I want you to take out some fresh paper, and, during the next period, write a review of the book you were supposed to have read. You have forty minutes. Ready? Start!"

They didn't say a word but picked up their pens.

As they passed my desk on the way out to hand in their papers, they all wished me "Shabbat Shalom!", a happy Sabbath, with what seemed like new respect.

It felt good! Could I have carried this off two years ago?

When I came home from school that day, I found it in my box! The thick blue envelope from the U.S.

Hardly daring to breathe, I ripped it open.

"My darling Sylvia,
As you must have gathered, I am married. Can you ever forgive me for lying to you? I could not possibly have told you when I met you. Would you have gone away with me if I had? I stayed over in Paris for two days because I needed time to think things over. While there I made the firm decision to go back to my wife and children which is why I sent you that note. And I came back here to Philadelphia with every intention of forgetting you and returning to Fran. But,

I simply couldn't do it.

Those wonderful few sunlit days with you threw into stark relief the shabbiness, the drabness of my marriage. Let me explain the circumstances under which I married...."

He went on for twelve more pages describing how he had left what was then Palestine to study in the U.S. with very little money, how he had waited on tables to work his way through, how lost and lonely he had felt the first few years, how he had met Fran in college, had begun to date her, how her parents had "gobbled him up", never ceased making overtures to him, made him most welcome in their home, offered to put him through a Master's program in engineering. He knew he was far from being madly in love with Fran, but he did respect her parents who were well-to-do. He realized that they were eager to have him as a son-in-law and that he could do far worse. He kept hoping he'd fall in love with Fran on the way, but this had not happened. Their marriage had merely become a framework within which to raise their two children. He was now determined to get out. In a long talk with Fran, even she had agreed that the marriage left a lot to be desired, and she was no more happy in it than he was. She would not fight him on the divorce. He had already moved out, he underlined. It was merely a question of remaining separated from Fran for a year and a half. Then he'd get his divorce, and he and I would be married.

"A year and a half isn't so long, darling, and we will have the rest of our lives ahead of us. Sylvia, you and I are so compatible. We have so much in common, have so much to talk about, have so much fun together. I know we'll have a happy and successful marriage. Please come back, darling. Come back right away! I need you. I can't tell you how much. I promise you, darling, everything will work out. We *will* be married. To quote Hertzl. 'If you will it, it is no dream!'"

I was dumbfounded.

Never in my wildest dreams had I imagined I would ever get such a letter from anyone. I was delirious with joy! He loved me! He had enjoyed me! He had been as happy with me as I was with him -so happy he was willing to turn his entire life upside down for me!

Then my conscience began to gnaw at me. I could not take him from his wife and his children who were only six and eight. I tried to think what my father would advise. And I remembered something he had once told me. Edith had said at the end that she had always known in her heart that nothing would come of their romance because, "You can't build your happiness on someone else's unhappiness."

My thoughts did a somersault. I couldn't afford not to take up with Norman. I had had such appalling luck with men. I might never meet anyone who loved me like that again. Whom I loved so much. No. I couldn't give him up. It was too much to ask of flesh and blood.

My thoughts swiftly turned around again. Hadn't I heard and read a thousand times that married men never, but never, leave their wives for the "other woman". What if he never intended to get a divorce! I would remain forever something he had in New York "on the side"! I could waste my whole life waiting!

My feelings became completely snarled.

Everything now depended on the kind of letter I wrote Norman. I planned and planned it. I rewrote it nine times. I read it to Pam. I kept changing the wording.

In the end, I sent Norman a loving letter telling him I was delighted to hear from him and that I had enjoyed our transcending few days so much that I did forgive him. Still, I could not bring myself to break up his marriage since his children were so young. It would be so much better if I did not return this June. I suggested that, if he were truly serious about getting a divorce, I would wait for him. Then, when the divorce became final, I'd be more than happy to return to the U.S. and resume our relationship. I was testing the strength of his feeling for me.

Norman, apparently, needed precisely this challenge. He began bombarding me with letters three and four times a week. In twelve weeks, I received forty-two letters. I came home from work one day and was overwhelmed to find my bathtub filled with flowers!

I returned in mid-June.

*   *   *   *

Now we were savoring our first week-end in America together. I gazed again at Norman sleeping so contentedly in my bed, worn out from our strenuous night together. I smiled and stroked his soft hair. I couldn't believe he was actually here with me in my bed. Mine! How did I get so lucky?

I was not to feel lucky long.

Things I found vaguely disturbing began to crop up in our relationship. I kept brushing them away as one brushes away flies.

One morning over breakfast about three weeks after my return, Norman startled me by asking, "Do you have any money?"

"What do you mean, money?"

"You must have some. You'll have a pretty good job in the fall. You probably got a decent divorce settlement. Your father's doing well in real estate."

I felt a trickle of nausea run down my throat.

"You need money?"

"Not for myself. But my younger brother in Israel wants to buy a gas station. I'd like to help him out."

There was something slimy underfoot, and I was slipping.

Was there anything wrong with Norman asking me? I couldn't be sure. I knew it *felt* wrong.

My stomach began to cramp as it so often did when I was with my mother.

"I'd love to help you, dear, but as a matter of fact, I walked out with only the tiniest divorce settlement."

"I don't believe you."

What was going on here? Why was he acting as if I owed him something? What should I do now? What would a really clever girl do?

This was awful. But I mustn't risk antagonizing him. I needed him too much. "Darling," I defended myself, "I'm completely self-supporting. I don't get money from my father. Besides, he's no longer working. My parents live on their savings."

He shot me an angry look. "Fran's family not only put me through my Master's program, they helped my older brother study music in Switzerland. For three years!"

What was he doing? Setting up a competition between me and Fran? I couldn't cope with this. But I continued pretending all was well even to myself. I put my arm through his. "Aw, honey, don't be mad."

This quarrel, if you could call it a quarrel, marked the puncturing of my first illusion about Norman.

It was followed by many others.

Norman usually caught a four thirty bus out of Philadelphia on Friday night, arriving at my home in Brooklyn Heights about six thirty. One Friday a few months later, he did not turn up till after eight.

"What happened, darling?" I asked. "I was so worried."

He seemed in a foul mood. "It's Fran," he said sarcastically. "She's lost weight. So she wanted two hundred dollars to buy some new clothes. I had to go to the bank for it tonight."

"Just a minute," I said, trying to grasp what I was hearing. "Didn't you tell me Fran had worked for several years? And she has no money under her own name?"

"No. It's all under mine."

"She has no access to it?"

"No."

He had walked out on Fran and the two kids and left her without money! I tried not to show how shocked I felt.

"I give her a weekly allowance."

Again that trickle of nausea.

"Why are you putting me through the wringer about this, Syl? Since when is it your business?"

I wanted to say, "If I'm thinking of marrying you, don't you think it's important that I know your character?" But, of course, I didn't dare say it. Instead, I clenched my fists. I had been wrong to question him. It was stupid of me. And maybe he was right to be angry. But was he? Why was he putting me on the defensive? Why was he being so aggressive about this? Why was he sabotaging our relationship?

There could only be one answer. He had fallen out of love with me. So quickly! He found me irritating and unlovable and no longer cared whether he pleased me or not.

But was that the real reason? I kept staring at him. Slowly, his face grew blurred like faces seen under water. I put my arm around him. "I'm sorry, darling. I was out of line. I won't do it again!" I made him a lovely dinner to placate him.

The edifice began to crumble. I grew more and more unhappy.

Normally, Norman and I spent every week-end in my apartment, rarely going out, except perhaps for Saturday night dinner. About a year later, he arrived on a Wednesday. "Come on. I'll take you dancing at the Rainbow Room."

My eyes popped. I knew Norman had little money, and I didn't expect such treats.

"The Rainbow Room! Oh! That's beautiful! I'd love to go! But are you sure you can afford it! I think it's pretty expensive."

He grinned.

Dancing with Norman was a delight. I hadn't known he could dance so smoothly. He was full of surprises.

While we were dancing, he dropped the bomb, "This will be the last time I'm coming in, Syl," he crooned in my ear without missing a step. "I found someone else to sleep with!"

So I had lost Norman.

In my heart, I had always known I would. And he had been my last hope.

With the loss of Norman, I knew there was no point in going on. Nothing in my entire life had ever gone right. It would be so much better to end it.

I left a note only for my father, asking his forgiveness.

The following Friday night, at the outset of the July fourth week-end, I told anyone who would possibly call me that I was going away for a few days. Then, sure that I'd get no phone calls to wake me, I took every sleeping pill in the house. Thirty-eight of them.

* * * *

I awoke with profound shock to find I was still alive!

My mouth felt dry and bitter. My lips were parched. My legs contorted. I could hardly move. But I was alive!

It was not only a shock to find myself alive. It was a cruel betrayal. I could not go back to my past bleak life. I had no life to go back to!

But was I really alive? How could I be sure this was not just one more of my sardonic dreams? Like the familiar dream of just missing a train by a minute. Or of asking people directions in a strange city and finding they spoke a foreign language and didn't understand me. Or finding myself going up on a down escalator so that, no matter how fast I walked, I stayed in the same place.

No. If I was dreaming, that meant I was alive.

Harsh sunlight poured in through the window. I had been prepared for the world to end. But it had gone on.

Talk about being inept! I was so inept I had failed even at suicide. One of my ex-husband Henry's typical comments to me used to be, "Only a jerk like you would get poison ivy on my vacation." Or "Only a jerk like you would pick a restaurant that...." Whatever. Now I could hear him snickering, "Only a jerk like you would fail even at committing suicide."

But, then, if I hadn't been so inept, my life would not have been so intolerable to begin with, and I wouldn't have needed to commit suicide.

I got lost in my own reasoning.

The trouble was I was too hungry to think clearly.

I looked in the refrigerator. No food at all. I had not bought any food the last few days. There had seemed no point.

How long had I slept?

What day was this?

How could I find out? I'd ask someone. Dizzy and weak, I wobbled out of my apartment and out of my building. Hicks Street was empty. I turned the corner and found dozens of people milling about on Clark Street near the St. George Hotel. Could I ask someone? No. It was impossible! Just imagine being approached by a total stranger on the street asking you what day it was! What would you think?

I bought a newspaper at the kiosk.

The paper told me it was Monday. The clock over the Reception Desk at the hotel read half past two in the afternoon.

I had slept more than two and a half days!

At the hotel Coffee Shop, I first ordered a double chocolate milk shake because I was so thirsty. While drinking it, I motioned to the waiter behind the long, white counter. "I want three sandwiches."

"What kind? We have cheese, ham and cheese, chicken salad, tuna..."

"Doesn't matter."

The waiter who had a face like a bulldog with eyes to match, exchanged glances with the other, younger waiter as if to say, "Did you ever see a weirdo like this?"

The second waiter replied out loud, "Ah, this hotel's full of them."

*　*　*　*

I ate and ate.

Why had I not died?

God!

He wished me to stay alive for his own reasons.

I had never particularly believed in God up to now. But from this moment on, somehow I did.

Could all this mean God wanted me to stay alive for some purpose? That he had something better in store for me?

Part 5

Changing Direction

Chapter 11

The following day, Tuesday, I received a phone call from my friend, Amy.

"Hi, Syl. How was your trip to Boston?" Her cheery voice rang through the wires.

Was that what I had told her just before the July Fourth week-end?

"Okay."

"Just okay?"

"Look, Amy, it didn't turn out quite as I'd planned."

"Mysterious, huh?" I said nothing. "You sound strange, Syl. Listen, I'm going to Chester's this week-end. Why don't you come, too?"

Nowadays, unattached people meet in singles bars. In the fifties and sixties, they met at resorts. Chester's had the reputation of being "intellectual", a rung above the other Catskill resorts.

"Amy, I'm much too depressed."

"Aw, come on."

"There's no point in going if I'm depressed, Amy. I'll attract no one."

"But it's just what you need. It'll help you get over Norman."

"Amy, you know I hate parties because I dread being a wall-flower. Just think how much worse it must feel to be a wallflower for an entire week-end."

Amy's voice lilted. "Honey, this just might be the week-end you'll meet Mr. Right!"

I laughed sourly.

I admired Amy for her incurable optimism. Yet, I was struck by the ironies in her life. At thirty-eight, just a year older than I, Amy was slim, blond, pretty, sensuous, vivacious, warm-hearted, and always falling in love. I envied her for all the delightful qualities she had that I lacked.

But some crucial ingredient must have been missing. For she

seemed just as programmed to fail as I was.

Having had an extremely lonely childhood with elderly parents, she had always wanted a large family of her own so she'd "never be lonely again," and, at eighteen, had plunged into marriage with a talented violinist, Sol, whose lovemaking sent her into rhapsodies.

Amy had very quickly had two children she adored. She had felt confident that this would sway Sol from his fanciful and unrealistic dream of becoming a concert violinist and anchor him to his pedestrian job to support his family. But, one day, Sol had simply walked out. Amy was devastated.

Even now, many years later, she was still unaware that at the time of their marriage, there had been an implied promise that she would support him till he had fulfilled his dream. That their hidden agendas had collided.

Amy's second husband also turned out to be a man whose goals and lifestyle clashed with hers. Since this second divorce, every relationship had ended in fiasco. Yet, Amy remained buoyant and ever hopeful.

"Amy, you're wonderful! Where do you get the courage to keep trying?"

"Can't afford not to," she said flippantly. Then, her voice came back to earth. "Look, Syl, I don't know about you. But when I'm without a man for a long time, I get sort of icky."

I smiled at her honesty.

"And I think you do, too, Syl, only you don't know it yet. Why don't you come? It'll do you a world of good."

* * * *

Amy liked to "operate" alone and disappeared the moment we arrived at Chester's, leaving me to my own devices.

Even as I approached my table for Friday night dinner, I knew the week-end was doomed. I had packed mostly dressy clothes and was wearing an outfit Norman had admired on me - a black velvet skirt and an uncluttered black nylon top with a deep Vee front and back that accentuated my figure. Only now did I realize people didn't dress *up* at Chester's. They dressed *down*. On this hot July evening, everyone looked cool and casual in pastel cotton blouses and skirts. I sat down at the large round table and, too embarrassed to meet anyone's eye, munched on one carrot stick after another from the communal bowl. And I don't even like carrots!

"Big crowd, tonight," murmured the balding man on my left. He had a long face and intense blue eyes behind thick glasses. His remark was perfectly ordinary. But there was something non-threatening about it and him that made my tensions gradually fall away.

We began to chat and continued talking afterwards on a long walk through the hotel grounds. My dinner partner seemed different from any man I had ever met. Instead of maneuvering to get me into bed as quickly as possible as all the others did, he encouraged me to talk about myself. I was starving for a shoulder to cry on, and found myself pouring out confidences I had never told any other man - about the kind of lover Norman had been, about the kind of husband Henry had been, about George who proposed to me on the subway and married someone else before I could give him an answer, about my lifelong bad luck.

He kept listening, his face showing deep interest and empathy.

"You're listening to me as though you're a therapist," I joked.

"I am."

"You are?"

"Well, I used to be a Rabbi. But I decided I could help more people as a therapist so I got more training. I'd like to help you. I feel I can."

"I've had bad luck with therapists, too."

A slight smile crossed his face. "What kind of help do you think you need most?"

I thought a long minute. Finally, I burst out, "I keep falling in love with the wrong man! I'd like you to teach me how to fall in love with the right man."

He raised his brows. "You're on." He gave me his card.

"Give me two and a half years, and I'll give you a new life."

"Promise?" I smiled.

"Promise. Well, I can almost promise. A lot depends on you."

Somehow, I believed him. "I think I'll take you up on that, Dr....?"

"I'm not a doctor. Call me Amos."

* * * *

I began to see Amos the following Wednesday.

"What do you think all your men have had in common?" Amos had fixed his intense gaze on me. "You tell me there were at least three?"

"Y-yes."

"Then, you see there was a pattern. What did they all have in common?"

"I don't know. They were all so completely different from one another."

"Yes. But there was a pattern. There was one thing they all had in common. What was it?"

I felt I was wringing my brain dry. "I don't know."

"Sylvia, try hard to think what they had in common."

"Honest, I don't know."

"What did they all lack?"

"Lack?"

"Yes. What did they all lack?"

"I don't know."

"The ability to love!" He waited for that to sink in.

I felt the earth move under me. "Yes!" I cried. It was like finding the lost chord!

"And why do you think you were always so unaware of that lack?"

I remained deep in thought. My head was beginning to ache with the effort. "Because I never expected...anyone to l-love me."

"Wonderful! Go on. Why did you never expect it?"

"Because I felt so...un-unlovable." I whispered.

"Exactly. It makes perfect sense, doesn't it? By whom is a person who feels unlovable irresistibly magnetized?"

I sat with my mouth open. "What?"

"By someone who is unable to love!"

I began to breathe very quickly. "Y-yes, I see that."

"Now," he seemed to be probing into my soul. "Why do you feel so unlovable?"

My heart was pounding. My eyes brimmed. "It has to do with..."

"Yes, Sylvia, go on."

"With..." I wet my dry lips.

"Go on"

"With my relationship with my mother!" I exploded.

"Exactly. Over and over again you sought out men as unloving as your mother to see if you could make them love you. It's as if you were reliving your childhood again and again trying against all odds to make it come out right this time."

"You think all my men have been reincarnations of my mother?"

"Looks like it."

I thought for a long time.

"And I didn't meet them by accident but sought them out?"

"That's right."

"I find that hard to believe. How did I know when I met them?"

"People are attuned to each other's neuroses. The bully finds the victim. The person who likes to dominate finds the one who enjoys being dominated. It's also what he's used to."

"So I was looking for what I was used to. Someone as unloving as my mother. A comfortable, or rather uncomfortable, old shoe."

"That's exactly right."

I walked out in a daze.

Chapter 12

"All right," Amos crossed his legs and sat back in his chair when I came in the following week. His blue gaze pierced me. He was waiting for me to begin.

"You want me to start talking about my mother."

He shrugged. "What do you think?"

"I know I should. That's why I'm here. But it's so hard."

"Why?"

"Because."

"Because why?"

"It's - painful. It's like p-pulling off a scab."

"Who put the scab there?"

"I did."

"Why?"

"Because. Because I couldn't -"

"Yes? You couldn't?"

He watched me and waited.

"It's all so hard to remember."

He kept his eyes on me.

"It's like I buried everything."

"Because?"

"Because it was so painful. Because it hurt so much." I was near tears.

"Sylvia, the feelings and memories we bury are those which control our lives."

I swallowed that. "Yes."

"You were talking about the pain."

"Yes. It's so difficult to talk about it. I think I've kept myself from remembering a lot because I couldn't bear the pain."

"And how do you think you're going to get over the pain?"

I thought a moment. "You're going to say by talking about it."

"By bringing it up to your consciousness."

"Yes." I sat still, trying to look back into my childhood.

There was a very long pause.

"Want me to help you remember?"

"Yes."

"All right. Tell me your earliest memory."

"At what age?"

"I don't know," he shrugged. "Three. Four."

"I don't have any early memories. We lived in Istanbul till I was about three. I only know what I've been told. My father had an important job with the Steamship Company, I had severe dysentery as an infant. But I have no real memories."

"All right. Focus in on when you were, say, eight. Where were you living then?"

"Montreal."

"Describe your house."

"It was on Esplanade Avenue near Mt. Royal. It had a long drab outside stairway and was on the third floor. It was a long railroad flat. My father also had an office there for his lubricating oil business. But we were so poor we had virtually no furniture. Except for the shabby old piano that was always out of tune."

"Yes? You had a piano?"

I nodded. "In fact, my earliest Montreal memory concerns that piano. I can still hear my mother telling my father, "Sylvia will never be pretty. We'll just have to give her piano lessons."

"What was going through your mind just now as you said that?"

"How much I hated the piano lessons and the piano. The mere fact that my mother was forced to give me piano lessons she could not afford, despite the fact that I was so unmusical, only showed me how ugly I really was, and to what desperate lengths she had been driven to compensate for it."

Amos raised his brows.

"Worst of all, I never learned to play. I just had no talent. My mother never let me forget it. After all, we had money for neither the piano nor the lessons."

There was a long pause.

"Since the piano was the symbol of your ugliness, how could you possibly have been enthusiastic about it?"

My jaw dropped. "You mean -"

Amos nodded slowly.

* * * *

Another session with Amos.

I sat and stared at him. I had no ideas. Then, I met his eyes.

"Want to try a memory when you were nine?"

I thought a moment. "Nine I can't remember just yet. But I remember ten."

"Okay. Let's do ten."

"My mother and I were coming out of a shoe store on Park Avenue. I hated to buy shoes. My mother never failed to tell me what big feet I had and how small her feet were. Well, we were just coming out of the shoe store when we met a woman from my mother's organization. The Pioneer Women. A top heavy woman with a bumpy nose.

"I can still remember that conversation."

"'Hello, Mrs. Berman,' she said. 'So this is your big daughter. My, how she's grown!'

"'Hello, Mrs. Lifshitz,' my mother lilted in her company voice. 'Sylvia, say 'hello',' she nudged me.

"I stood there, wanting to sink through the sidewalk.

"My mother shrugged and sighed. 'You see how she is? I don't know what's the matter with her. She doesn't know how to talk to people!'"

"Now that you look back, how do you feel about that story, Sylvia?"

"What do you mean?"

"You told the story. But you gave very few feelings."

"I did. I said I wanted to sink into the ground."

"Because?"

"Because I was so - embarrassed - ashamed."

"Why were you so embarrassed and ashamed?"

"Why do you think? Because I had no poise. I never knew how to talk to people. It was always happening to me. It still does."

He lit a cigarette. "How does a child acquire poise?"

I was startled. "What?"

"Do young children know how to speak to people?"

"I don't think they care what people think of them."

"That's very interesting. And because they don't care what happens?"

"I don't know."

"Because they don't care, they are spontaneous and free. Which is one of the chief charms of children."

"Yes."

"Was there ever a time when you felt spontaneous and free?"

I found that question painful. "I don't know. I'd have to think. Maybe. In Istanbul. Actually, I have a fleeting image of something. I see it. Then it goes away."

"Great! Tell me about the image."

"Oh, I don't know, Amos. It's just a fragment. Connected to nothing."

"Go on."

"It's silly. It's just being on the floor, I guess. Among women's legs."

"Legs with stockings or bare legs?"

"Bare legs, I think."

"Go on, Sylvia."

"I don't know any more."

There was a long pause.

"What's your feeling about that memory."

"Happy. No. Sad. Oh, I don't know."

"Anything else you can tell me about that memory?"

"No. But I have another one. Even vaguer. It's about being high up."

"High up where?"

"I don't know. On a hill, maybe."

"Go on."

"I can't Amos. Really. Can't we go on to something else?"

"Sure. Maybe these memories will come back to you another day. They might be very valuable. Okay. Let's go back to when you were ten. You were no longer spontaneous and free. Right?"

"I was the most self-conscious child in the world."

"Sylvia, every young child is spontaneous and free. How do you suppose you became so self-conscious?"

"I'm not sure."

"Let's try it another way. Why do you think you were so **self-conscious?**"

"Oh, that! Well, let's see. I guess I was sure that if I let down my guard for a minute, I'd say something foolish."

"And why would you suppose that?"

I stared at him. "M-my mother was always telling me how stupid I was." My voice sounded hoarse.

"Can you take that a step further?"

"What do you mean?"

"Can you see that it was your mother who curbed your spontaneity?"

"H-how?"

"You tell me."

"By telling me to say 'hello'?"

"Yes. What did that show?"

"That she didn't trust me to know what to say - to handle myself."

"Excellent." He smiled at me. "It's up to parents to encourage their children. Give them confidence. Your mother did the reverse. No wonder you were ill at ease." He paused. "One thing more. Since when does a child, or for that matter any human being, have to be perfect to be worthy of love?"

I let out a deep sigh of relief. Suddenly, I felt as if a great weight had been lifted off my shoulders.

* * * *

"You know what I notice when you describe these memories?" said Amos a few months later. "You never show any anger at your mother."

I turned red.

"What's going through your mind right now, Sylvia?"

I bit my nails. "I don't know. I guess I just never felt angry with her."

He waited for me to say more. When I didn't, he said, "And why was that?"

I thought a long time. Then I took a deep breath. "I felt it was too dangerous."

"Why?"

"My position with her was so - precarious. I couldn't afford to lose what little attention I got."

"Sylvia, can you agree that you had a right to be angry? That you deserved to be treated much better than you were. That every human being does. The same thing happened with Norman, didn't it? Don't you see the pattern?"

"I don't know."

"Let me rephrase that question, as they say in court. Can you think of any time in your childhood when you were angry at your mother?"

I reached deep into my memory. "No, not really. Wait. Maybe. Yes. I can think of one time when I was nearly angry."

"Let's hear."

"I was about twelve. My mother and I were invited to a Bar Mitzvah. At the dinner, my mother sat with the adults while I was seated at the teenagers' table, the youngest person there. I was ill at ease for the longest time as the gay banter flew around me. I was just beginning to loosen up and enjoy myself when my mother, mindful of her motherly duties, suddenly, appeared behind me.

'Sylvia,' she stage whispered so loudly she could be heard across the large round table. 'You don't eat fish with a knife!"

I was so flooded with shame, I wanted to die on the spot. I

could not utter another word or look anyone in the eye the rest of the day. For one split second, my head was on fire with hatred of my mother and anger at her."

I shuddered. "Amos, as I sit here I can still feel them coursing through me."

I sat perfectly still, shivering, reliving that moment, writhing with the embarrassment of it, breathing heavily.

"I can't talk any more, Amos." I got up quickly. "I just can't."

I ran out of the session.

For the next few weeks, I avoided this subject. But, about a month later, when I sat silent for a long time, Amos asked,

"What's on your mind today, Sylvia?"

"I was thinking of the day I ran out of here."

"You want to talk about that day now?"

"Yes. No. I don't know." I paused, then blew out all the rest of the sentence on one breath. "I ran out because it was so hard to talk about how I had felt that day at the Bar Mitzvah."

Amos kept his eyes on me. "You said that for a split second you felt anger and hatred for your mother. What did you do with them?"

I looked down at the floor. "I - throttled them. I couldn't afford the luxury."

"You throttled them because you couldn't afford the luxury. Do you think there may have also been another reason?"

"What?"

"You tell me."

Some weeks later I came up with the answer.

"I had to stifle the anger because I was afraid of what I might do to her if I allowed myself to feel it."

"Wonderful! And how do you feel as you say that?"

"Just awful!" I shivered. "It's terrifying."

"Okay. Let's see where that terrifying thought led you."

"What do you mean?"

"You were determined to stifle the anger in you. Right?"

"Yes."

"And what was the most effective way you could do that?"

"I already told you. By burying everything."

"You did more than that. Think about it."

I avoided the subject during my next few weeks of therapy. But some months later, I returned to it.

"I've been trying to think how I managed to stifle my anger at my mother."

"What would have been the most effective way to stifle it?"

"That question has been torturing me for weeks."

"And?"

I sat and thought. "I think I just may have stumbled on something. I think - I *think* I had to convince myself that the fault lay with me. Not with her."

"Bravo! Go on."

"That, if she disapproved of me, it was because there was something to disapprove of. I still feel that way, you know."

"What?"

"That there's something wrong with me. And that's why she couldn't love me."

"She couldn't love you because you were, shall we say, defective in some way. Is that what you're saying?"

"Yes."

"But that's precisely why you've been living with such a low self-concept all these years. Because you had to convince yourself that all the fault lay with you. Because you were terrified of what you might do if you dared put the blame on her."

"Yes."

"How do you feel about that?"

"I think you're right. It was much easier - and safer to put the blame on myself than to go against my mother's authority."

For the next few weeks, we kept returning to the subject again and again.

"So you think I have such a low self-concept because I found that easier to live with than putting the blame on my mother."

"Yes. And for other reasons."

"What?"

"You tell me."

"I understand why I had to put the blame on myself. But in addition, all my life, she's never stopped telling me how defective I am."

"And why did you believe her?"

"Because she was my mother."

Amos smiled. "What made her such a big expert on your character?"

I stared at him. I had no answer.

"You see she brainwashed you. And you brainwashed yourself. You played right into her ploy."

"What ploy?"

"I'm not sure. I think she desperately needed to feel superior to you."

I had to chew that over for a few weeks.

"How do I raise my self-concept?" I asked one day.

"Good question. I've been waiting for you to ask. By realizing your mother was wrong. By not believing her."

The room was spinning around me.

"By not believing her!" I repeated.

"That's right."

"But that's so hard."

He shrugged.

"I always believed her. I took - accepted what she said about me completely - hook, line, and sinker. I still hear her tape in my head."

"I know you do. If you want to have a better self-concept, you must *erase* her tape."

"How do I do that?"

"By just doing it."

I heaved a deep sigh.

Some months later, I asked Amos.

"One thing puzzles me. You seem to want me to be angry at my mother. Why is that?"

"Sylvia, you must detach from her. You must! You'll never have a better life till you do. She will always have the power to upset you and to pull you back into your old self-concept. But you'll never be able to detach unless you have the anger to give you the impetus."

"How can I detach from her? I love my father. He's been ill. I want to see him from time to time. That means seeing her."

"Detaching emotionally is far more important than detaching physically. If you manage to detach yourself emotionally, it won't matter if you see her once in a while. She'll never be able to hurt you again."

I was, finally, beginning to understand.

"It's not the anger that's important, Sylvia. It's the detachment."

I felt every syllable tap like a little hammer into my brain.

* * * *

Nevertheless, for the next several months, I kept spewing out my anger at my mother, now that I had permission to do so. It felt so good. Of course, I only spewed it out to Amos. I pretty much avoided my real mother.

"You never wanted to murder her?" Amos asked one day.

I thought a moment. "No."

"Why not? Lots of teenagers have strong desires to kill parents for less."

"Well, my whole problem lay in my lack of self-esteem. How would becoming a murderess enhance my self-esteem?"

Amos grinned.

"Amos, I feel I've got to get past this anger and hatred. How long am I going to keep talking about it? I mean, for the past few months, I've hated my mother with a passion. It was absolutely wonderful to - to vent - to siphon off all the rage I had stored up in me. It's like all my life I had lived with a silent scream in my throat. And I desperately needed to howl my pain to the sky.

"But I don't want to get stuck on the howling. It's destructive. After a while, it no longer helps. I don't want to be a person who hates. It's hard to live with hatred. It's - ugly. It's - corroding. It hurts you more than the person you hate. It gets in the way of good relationships."

Amos beamed. "You're basically a very healthy person, Sylvia. You've a healthy core. That's your relationship with your father coming out."

I nodded. "I feel that my hatred and anger that used to be suppressed crippled me. And now that it's more out in the open, it's still crippling me. Amos, I have to let go of it!"

"I think it's wonderful that you've gotten to this place so fast, Sylvia. Because if you want to meet the kind of people you should be meeting, people who are able to love, you can only attract them if you are also that kind of person. If you let go of the hatred and bitterness and rage."

"I know. I know. But how do I let go of them, Amos?"

"By just letting go. It's like stopping smoking."

I must have looked incredulous. "You make it sound easy."

"Of course, it's not easy. Most worthwhile things are not. Let me explain what's involved. Can you describe a well-adjusted person?"

"Oh, we've talked about that till I'm blue in the face. Someone who's filled with love, not hatred. Someone who's optimistic and not pessimistic and bitter. Someone who's able to show warmth and whose emotions are not all frozen up as mine have been."

"And how do they get that way?"

I sighed. "By being loved as a child - loved the right way."

"Yes. But such a person also usually has a good role model to emulate - generally a mother or father or both. It's important to have someone of the same sex, if possible. We both know what your mother was like. And your father, while he knew how to love and did love you in his own way, really couldn't cope very well with his own life. He was rarely able to stand up to your mother about you. I'm afraid he really wasn't a very good role model either."

"He was too afraid of my mother for all those early years to be effective. He loved people and helped so many people in his life. He was such a kind person. But he was very cruel to my mother."

"All right. So here we are. You're nearly forty. You can't redo your childhood, unfortunately. And you don't have a good role model. So - where do we go from here?"

"I don't know."

"Sylvia, you have to create your own role model to emulate."

"What? How do you mean?"

"Sylvia, I want you to try very hard to focus on the kind of life you would have if you let go of the anger and hatred, on the kind of person you would be."

I wrestled with that for a few weeks.

"If you keep focusing on the new Sylvia you will be if you let go," Amos kept telling me, "YOU WILL BECOME THAT PERSON."

* * * *

On my last visit to him, Amos said, "Now, I want you to look back to your childhood and visualize the child you were then. Pick an age, six, eight. Can you see the little Sylvia?"

I gulped. "Yes."

"Describe the child you see."

I kept remembering pictures I had seen of myself and also remembering how I had felt. "Oh, she's wistful - and - has big, hungry eyes."

My eyes filled.

"Sylvia, I want you, the adult, happier Sylvia to take that little girl in your arms and hug her. Because she had nobody."

I burst into tears.

Chapter 13

Within three years, I had become a totally different person. Amos suggested I stop seeing him. I had changed from being a girl who felt personally unlovable and felt that the world was a place from which one must not expect happiness, to being a person who felt worthwhile and loveable and felt that the world was a place where all kinds of good things lay in store for her.

All my life, I had lain in bed as long as possible each morning, dreading to launch each new day.

Now, I felt as if a new sun had burst in the sky, giving me a buoyancy and a zest for life I had never dreamed possible. I could not wait to greet each day.

My entire dating pattern changed.

I was already in my late thirties, a time when all men of the right age were reputed to be either married or unmarriageable. Every unattached woman I knew was complaining bitterly of a male shortage. Yet, to my own never ending amazement, now that I was a happier person, more and more able to show warmth, fine men, men who were able to love, were crawling out of the woodwork to meet me.

In the ensuing three years, I met and dated several, and, finally, chose to marry one of them. I was not quite forty-three.

I detached successfully from my mother. Just how successfully can be gauged from what happened when I first told her about Bernie.

I had called her to find out how my father was. He had suffered yet another small stroke.

After bewailing my father's condition and the boring, confined life she was leading because of it, my mother asked with a sigh, "And what are your plans for the summer?"

For years now, I had not answered such questions on the theory that the less my mother knew about my activities, the less there was for her to criticize. But I was beginning to feel more secure.

"I'm doing something totally different this time, Ma. I'm going camping. In a forest. In the Allegheny mountains. For two weeks."

"Are you crazy? You're going camping in a forest all alone?"

"I didn't say I was going alone. I'm going with a man. His name is Bernie."

"Are you crazy? You're going all alone to a forest with a total stranger?"

There was a long pause while I gathered courage for what I wished to say.

"What are you worried about, Ma? You're afraid he'll rape me?"

My mother sputtered. "Well, of course. I've never heard of anything so - what girl in her right mind -"

"But Ma," I said softly. " He couldn't possibly rape me." I paused for effect. "I'm too willing."

This conversation marked my emancipation from my mother.

*　*　*　*

I had met Bernie at Tarleton, a larger, more elegant Chester's, in New Hampshire, that presented excellent intellectual programs with fine speakers. If, in the late sixties, you were an older, educated Jewish single who didn't enjoy the glitzy Concord, Tarleton was the place to be.

Saturday morning, I fell into conversation with an attractive young woman with a charming accent and the unusual name of Sigrid who told me that her parents were Survivors of the Holocaust from Poland, that they had escaped to Iceland where she had been born and had grown up. For many years she had loved Iceland where the people had been so kind to her and her family. But, after a while, she had begun to find the tininess and the homogeneity of Iceland stifling. Sigrid hated being "tucked away in a corner of the world where nothing ever happened." She longed for the diversity and excitement one can only find in a place like New York where she was living now. Her problem was that she was engaged to a fine

Icelandic doctor who did not wish to raise his children in "brutal America". He was attached to Iceland and refused to leave. She couldn't decide what to do. She asked what I thought.

I asked her how long she had been living in New York. She smiled, "four exhilarating months." I suggested first of all that she try New York for at least a year or two. While New York is all she says it is, she might find that, after a while, she missed the warmth of Iceland. She, herself, might wish to return. Sigrid sighed and shook her head. My next suggestion was that, if she did decide to return and accede to her fiance's wishes, it was extremely important that she didn't then resent her husband for the rest of her life which would ruin the marriage. If she made the decision to return, she should do it with good grace.

Sigrid's chin trembled. She looked thoughtful, squeezed my hand, thanked me warmly, and walked away.

I remained standing, concerned about how troubled she appeared, when a slender man in his mid-fifties with a thicket of grizzled hair, turned to me.

"I couldn't help overhearing you. There aren't many women up here who, instead of squeezing out every second to make out with men, would waste their time trying to help another woman. And a stranger at that."

Despite my current good adjustment, I still found it so difficult to accept a compliment that I stood gaping at him.

He intuited this, and his eyes beneath his shaggy brows crinkled in a smile. "I guess the compliment shook you up. Perhaps you'd better sit down." He motioned me to the long sofa.

I giggled. "It was something I feel well qualified to help her with. It just happens that my parents lived through something very similar. My mother wanted to live in Israel with her family and never forgave my father for abducting her to America."

There was a pause. "I bet lots of people confide in you." His hazel eyes looked kind, but I sensed something more than kindness there. Something deeper.

"How do you know?"

"You have a quality."

Again I boggled.

"Oh, come on. That's not such a great compliment."

I collected myself. "Yes, people do confide in me. I guess they sense I'd enjoy helping them. It makes my life interesting."

"Can I make an appointment to tell you the story of *my* life?"

"I'd be delighted."

"You live in New York?"

"Brooklyn Heights."

"Terrific. It happens I have to leave here shortly. And I'll be in Mexico City all this week. We're setting up a branch of our engineering firm. How about a week from next Saturday?"

I smiled into his eyes. "Sounds great!"

He stood up. So did I. He shook my hand. "Bernie Grossman."

Having touched, neither of us wished to let go. We stood there shaking hands endlessly and grinning.

*   *   *   *

Bernie turned out to be a most unusual husband - a husband who understood his wife intuitively.

Very early in our relationship, I had found out why.

He had been the favored child in his original family. His brother, Joe, only eighteen months older, had been the rejected one.

The reason Joe was rejected by his parents seems horrendous in the light of what we know now. Joe was talented in many ways. He was such a good actor that he was a child star in the Yiddish theatre on Second Avenue. He was artistic, did wood carving, painted in oil. But - Joe could never learn to read. Of course, now we know that he was suffering from dyslexia. But, in the twenties when Joe was growing up, no one had ever heard of dyslexia. Certainly not Joe's immigrant parents. Joe was considered a "dumkopf".

There could be no greater disgrace in a Jewish family. The fact that Joe never managed to graduate even from elementary school placed him beyond the Pale. Joe's parents scolded him for being lazy and stubborn. They humiliated him, thinking that might give him incentive.

By contrast, Bernie, who had always been an excellent student and graduated college with honors, was the apple not only of his mother's but of his father's eye.

As Joe grew into his late teens, he struggled to find jobs. But his inability to read always stood in his way, especially during the depression when even college graduates were out of work.

Joe felt worthless. On Bernie's twenty-first birthday, he gave up. He jumped off a roof and committed suicide.

Bernie had always felt he and Joe were close. Forever after, he was to wonder, if Joe had been so unhappy, why had he never confided in him? If he, Bernie, had known how desperate Joe felt, he would have seen to it that his parents did not criticize him so harshly. He would have given Joe encouragement, helped him find solutions.

The fact that Joe had not confided showed Bernie he had clearly been giving off the wrong signals. He had basked in his parents' love and pride while Joe was being demolished. He had been so smug and self-absorbed that he had been unaware of his brother's pain.

For the rest of his life, Bernie blamed himself for not having been sensitive enough to his brother. This sensitized him to other people, especially people who had suffered. He has the keenest sense of injustice I've ever known and cannot bear to see anyone in pain.

Certainly, he was acutely sensitive to me and my needs. He understood the rejected child in me.

Amos had once told me that the greatest joy in life comes from feeling visible to someone and feeling accepted for what one is.

From the moment I met Bernie, everything fell into place. I felt secure and comfortable. His concept of me corresponded closely with my own new concept of myself. He saw my insecurities and the ways in which they manifested themselves. But he viewed them as something I'd outgrow with his help. He rooted for me. My mother had constantly criticized me for my flaws. I was a terrible housekeeper and cook. I didn't know how to talk to people. I was stupid.

Bernie had that rarest of all qualities, innate emotional wisdom (he was the only person I had ever met who had had a happy childhood), praised me for what he and I both wished me to become. Gradually, I gained poise and self-assurance. I became a much better cook, for instance. With his encouragement, I went back to school to get training as a Family Counselor. I wrote a book for teachers. I stopped being terrified of giving speeches and was able to promote the book.

Handling teenagers had always petrified me which was why I had been afraid to teach high school. I had never wanted children of my own fearing that, no matter how hard I tried not to, I would be sure to pass on to them the treatment my mother had meted out to me. In my mind, the whole mother-child relationship was fraught with danger.

But now that I had more insight into myself and Bernie's love gave me so much more faith in myself, I managed to overcome my trepidation and found the courage to undertake something that makes far more confident women quake. Help Bernie raise his teenage children.

Three years before I met him, Bernie's wife had died of cancer after a long, lingering illness which affected both her children most adversely.

It was far from easy to mother them. I got off to a rocky start and made many mistakes. But, in the end, Bernie felt I did very well with both children, especially with my stepson with whom I developed an excellent relationship. I felt good about myself.

* * * *

Had I met an Bernie a few years earlier, I would have sabotaged the relationship. I would have suspected that something must be seriously wrong with him if he so readily accepted me. The fact that I was able to respond positively to his love now, showed how healthy I had become.

Bernie and I had had a happy marriage for eight years when we received that call from my mother's super, and the bomb fell.

*　*　*　*

The morning after that night when Bernie and I had left the expensive restaurant dinner untouched and then sat in front of the fire discussing my mother, we both woke about the same time. We usually did, and we always touched at that moment. I suppose each of us wanted reassurance the other was there.

We went back to mulling over our problem.

"You're overreacting, darling," said Bernie. "You know that, don't you? This is not going to tear our marriage apart. I'm in this with you. We'll handle it together. Together, we'll find a way."

I was inexpressively grateful. "You're wonderful, darling," I kissed him. Then I lay back in his arms. "Bernie, we must visit a Home for the Blind immediately. I heard of an excellent one in Yonkers."

We both took time off from work and visited the Home. We were most impressed with it, but we were told they accepted people on two conditions only. One was that they must be willing to come. The other was that they had to be well-adjusted. In fact, they wanted a statement from a psychiatrist certifying that my mother was well-adjusted.

"My mother well-adjusted!" I groaned, my heart sinking, as we got into the car for our long drive home. "And a psychiatrist has to certify it no less! And she has to come of her own volition!"

"Maybe we can well-adjust her," said Bernie jokingly.

"Yeah. Fat chance."

He kept driving. Suddenly, a thought hit me that was so exciting that I poked his arm almost causing us to drive into a pole. "That's it, Bernie! We have to well-adjust her! We must! It's our only chance to get her into that Home!"

Bernie turned to me. "What are you talking about, Zvi? How

on earth could you do that?"

"There's only one way! Through love!"

"Zvi, that's crazy!" He kept shaking his head. "You've had this acrimonious relationship for what? Fifty-one years. More than half a century!"

"It may sound crazy, but you have a better plan?"

"No."

"Then we try it."

He concentrated on his driving, making a difficult left turn in traffic.

"Do you have even the vaguest idea where to start?"

"With Amos. I have to see Amos to get advice on how to handle her. Immediately! Today! I can't afford to make mistakes! And I have no time to lose!"

"Yeah! Maybe that's an idea. Maybe that's what you need! A tune up!"

Chapter 14

"So I decided there's only one thing to do, Amos. To try to 'well-adjust' her with love. But when I thought it through, I realized it meant getting involved with her all over again. I'd get sucked into another lousy, destructive relationship. Amos, after all the years and all the effort I put into detaching from her, the last thing I want is to wind up exactly where I started fifteen years ago. I didn't sleep a wink all night."

"Sylvia, I don't think it means getting 'sucked in'."

"You don't?"

"Look, I was delighted with your progress last time. That you were able to detach from her so successfully and, on top of that, were able to work through your anger and bitterness and come out on the other side a much happier person. It's something so few people are able to do. I consider you one of my most promising graduates." He looked at me approvingly.

"I did detach. You know that. I had gotten to the point where very little she said or did ever ruffled me. I was so proud of myself."

"I was proud of you, too."

"Amos, detaching from her originally took every ounce of energy and inner strength I didn't even know I had. But it was something I had to do and I did it. With your help, of course. But that was child's play compared to what faces me now. You see, fifteen years ago, I could do it because I didn't have to see much of her. Oh, I went to visit my father from time to time. My mother was nasty, but we really had little interaction. I made sure of that. Now we have a completely different set of circumstances. She's so helpless, and I *have* to be involved with her or I'll never win her over and get her to trust me. The odds against my succeeding are astronomical anyway. But I must make every effort to get her into that home. I have no other recourse. I'm terrified."

"Sylvia, you're missing the point. It's precisely because you wish to win her that you can't afford to get involved."

"Now you've lost me."

"If you allow yourself to get 'sucked in' as you put it, then you lose control of your own behavior. And then you cannot possibly behave as you should if you wish to help her change. Can you follow me?"

"Maybe. Yes."

"That's why it's more important than ever that you remain detached at this point."

"And how do I keep from being sucked in?"

"You will not be sucked in, Sylvia. Not if you are determined not to be. Look what you've already accomplished. What strength you have."

"You have such faith in me."

Amos smiled. "If you want to try to melt her resistance you must, in fact, do more than detach. You must learn to disconnect your own feelings."

"You say that as if it's easy."

"Whether or not it's easy, you have to do it. You have to forget the past completely. The two of you have no joint history."

"Just like that!"

"I'm telling you what you have to do. Let's continue. This is not a mother-daughter relationship. You are not her daughter. You are her nurse. And you're attempting to put a difficult, incapacitated old patient into good humor before going to the dentist for root canal. What would you do?"

I thought a long moment. "Cajole her. Placate her. Make her feel good about herself."

"Yes. Tell her what she wants to hear. What you think will please her. You know her much better than I. What do you think she wants to hear?"

"Compliments. She never says a good word to anyone, but she just loves compliments. She's the most negative person in the world, Amos. One of the problems is that not only must I melt her resistance so she'll want to go to the home, but that we must get a psychiatrist to certify that she's a well-adjusted person."

A look of disbelief crossed Amos's face.

"You see what I'm up against? Listen, if I want to turn her into a more positive person, it seems to me there's just one way to do it. I have to be very positive and enthusiastic and cheerful and sweet myself to be a role model for her."

"That's excellent, Sylvia. I'm afraid you have your work cut out for you."

"I think it would help if Bernie, being a man, paid her compliments as well. I'll have to tell him which ones."

"Now you must do all this while depersonalizing the relationship. No matter how you're tempted, you don't react personally to anything she says. It's like being a therapist," he smiled.

"There's another aspect to all this, Amos. She's as obstinate as a mule. Have you any suggestions on how to handle that?"

"Hm," said Amos, thinking. "What sort of things drive her into obstinacy?"

"Oh, she resents any suggestions we make or any advice we give her. For instance, she absolutely refuses to go to an ophthalmologist although she's almost blind."

"What reason does she give?"

"I think she's afraid we'll control her or try to dominate her so she simply says 'No' to everything we suggest."

Amos crossed his long legs and selected a pipe from the row of six on his pipe rack. He filled the pipe and slowly lit it.

"Remember that children's story about the sun and the wind? The wind tried to blow off the man's cloak, but the harder the wind blew the more tightly the man pulled his cloak about himself. Then, the sun came out. It shone on the man and warmed him up, and he took off his cloak of his own volition."

"Yeah. We're back to the story of the nurse and the patient who won't go to the dentist."

"It would help a lot if you understood her better. What was her position in her family of origin?"

"She was the oldest of thirteen children. The oldest daughter, that is."

"And what position did that put her into?"

"Oh, I see what you mean. She always had lots of responsibility looking after the younger children. She was in a dominant position."

"And what kind of person did she become because of that?"

"A very domineering person. She's been used to being in a leadership position her entire life. She dominated many of her younger brothers and sisters, and my father, and me. I used to think of her as a steam roller. Yes, I see what you're driving at. I can imagine how she feels now, suddenly relegated to an inferior position where her children tell her what to do. Amos, you've been really helpful. So - what should we do?"

"You tell me."

"Hm. Let me think. I suppose avoid anything that might possibly smack of control for the time being."

"I think so."

"And - let's see, what else? I guess we'll have to wait till we've improved the relationship, and she's learned to trust us." I sighed. "Oh, boy! Amos, it all seems so hopeless. My head aches just thinking what I'm up against."

"What have you got to lose? Try it and see how it works."

"It does seem awfully cold-blooded, though, doesn't it? I wanted to win her with love."

Amos looked at me with compassion. "But that's the whole point, Sylvia. If you're lucky, she may just perceive what you're giving her as love."

Bernie, who was twelve years older than I and on the verge of retirement, had planned to take a terminal leave for reasons of health in any event. We began to visit my mother every day and to show her our "love."

"Hello, Ma." We both kissed her. "We were in the neighborhood so we thought we'd drop in to see how you are."

"Suddenly, you're interested?"

"Of course, we're interested, Ma."

"Yeah! You're interested! Listen. Let me tell you about my

next door neighbor, that nasty Mrs. Rabinowitz. She's been spying on me!"

"I'm sorry she upset you, Ma."

"Each time I step out of the door, there she is. She followed me to the incinerator. I told her a thing or two. Believe me, she won't spy on me again." She glared at me. "I have a feeling somehow you're behind this."

Bernie and I exchanged a glance. Bernie rolled his eyes.

"Well," I said with determined cheerfulness. "Now that we're here, may we come in?"

"You're already in." My mother turned her back on us.

"We brought you some cake, Dvorah," said Bernie.

"Yes, I know how much you love chocolate cake, Ma."

My mother turned. Her face softened. "Chocolate cake?"

"Yes. You've always loved chocolate cake. I can still remember the cake you used to make when Mitch and I were small. I used to love licking the icing off the spoon. Here. Try some of this. Isn't it delicious?" I cut a small piece off and put it in her mouth. "Wait. I'll make some tea to go with it. Hot tea is so pleasant on a cold day." In the kitchen, I quickly picked some of the debris off the floor.

"What are you doing in my kitchen so long?" asked my mother in a harsh voice.

"Oh, she's just cleaning up a little," Bernie said .

"I don't need Zviah, of all people, to clean my kitchen for me. Some housekeeper she is! Does she ever make a bed in your house? When she was a girl you could never walk into her room! And she never lifted a finger to help me."

Bernie's lips twitched, but he made no answer.

"Zviah, get out of my kitchen!" She turned to Bernie. "God knows what a mess she'll leave."

I decided to disregard her comments and came in smiling broadly with the tea and cake on a platter.

"Here you are! Oo! This is such a yummy cake!"

"Wonderful cake!" Bernie smacked his lips, smiling at me behind his hand.

"Isn't it delicious, Ma?"

Ever since I had known my mother, she had never made one single positive comment about anything. Today, caught by our enthusiasm, I could see she was trying to, but she simply didn't know how.

"Y-yes," she managed.

"Oh, I'm so glad you enjoyed it."

"Who said I enjoyed it? I never said I enjoyed it."

"I could see by your face you did. We'll come again tomorrow and bring you more."

Bernie poked me. He was telling me he had never agreed to come *every* day. I telegraphed him a look which said we had to.

I was watching my mother's face. She looked bewildered.

"You're coming again tomorrow?"

"Sure."

"I don't understand. Why are you coming?"

"Now that Bernie's retiring we have more time. I'm taking time off from my job, too. We know how lonely you are since Pa died."

My mother's eyes blazed. "I don't need your pity! If you came out of pity, you can leave right now!" She stood up angrily.

I could sense Bernie gritting his teeth.

"Sit down, Dvorah. We came because we wanted to be with you."

I could feel something change in my mother. As though she was shifting gears.

"You're really coming again tomorrow?"

"Yes." I said.

My mother sighed. "Pa was sick so much the last years. He certainly was no company for me. And he had always been a terrible husband. But," she heaved a deep sigh, "I see now he was better than nothing."

My mother was not biting my head off as she usually did! She was actually talking to me for the very first time as if I were a human being!

Her eyes were filled with the past. "The day of the chess game, I knew then I should never have married him."

Bernie looked inquiringly at me. I shrugged.

"You took good care of Pa, Ma. You were always good at taking care of sick people."

She raised her chin proudly. "When I was a girl, I nursed all my brothers and sisters through cholera. I was the only healthy one."

"I know, Ma. You were the best of all the seven daughters."

It was as if I had tuned on a faucet.

"When I was not yet seven years old, I had to wash all the laundry for my mother's inn. Every Monday, summer and winter, I was given a hugh pile of laundry this high. I dragged it down to the river in Berdichev where we lived at the time and pounded it on the rocks. Even in the winter when I had to break through the ice and my hands froze. It took all day. I was so foolish in those days, I felt sure God was watching and would some day make it all up to me. That he'd give me a wonderful husband and a daughter who was as good to me as I had been to my parents." She realized she had gotten carried away. "Ah, what's the use of talking?" She shot me a disgusted look as if to say, "And look at the kind of daughter I wound up with!"

I pretended to notice nothing. "Ma, you look really nice, today."

"Yes," chimed in Bernie, who had been primed by me. "You must have been an unusually beautiful girl when you were young."

My mother did not answer. She sat very still, listening to us as if our words were music.

I sat smiling, allowing her to savor the moment.

"We have to go now, Ma. Would you tell us what you need so we can bring you groceries when we come tomorrow?"

"Oranges, bananas, potatoes," she said numbly.

"We're taking your garbage with us so you don't have to go to the incinerator," said Bernie.

We kissed her and left.

We had started these visits out of sheer desperation so she would be accepted into the Home for the Blind and would agree to go. At first, the odds had seemed a thousand to one against our succeeding. On this first visit, though she had denigrated me as usual, not once but many times, she had, nevertheless, dropped some of her armor toward the end.

On our next visit, she again made disparaging remarks about me to Bernie because I had refused to go to work at fourteen so Mitch could attend college. She described in detail how she had had to give him very special care since 'poor Mitch' had weighed just six pounds at birth. I, at the ripe old age of five, had not understood that and had been jealous. "She was actually jealous!" she repeated with bitterness. "Can you imagine? To throw tantrums just because the baby needed all my time!"

On the same day, however, she dropped even more of her armor.

By our third visit, my mother had mellowed so she was unrecognizable. Our crazy idea appeared to be succeeding beyond our wildest dreams.

At the same time, I discovered there was a four to six month waiting period at the Home for the Blind.

"I can't keep up this facade for six months, Bernie. The strain is already driving me crazy. I know how you must feel."

"How I feel? At first, quite frankly, I thought it was sheer hell to go out there and do my Academy Award performances. I can think of one or two better things to do with my time and, let's face it, your mother is hardly an engaging personality."

I mustered a smile. "It's a very loving thing to do, Bernie. I'm sure you know how much I appreciate it. I don't think I could go through all this if I didn't have your moral support."

"I know that, darling. What I was getting to was that, if I didn't feel we were making headway, you couldn't drag me out there. But, Zvi, you have to admit we're succeeding with her where we never in a million years imagined we would. Slowly. But there's a real trend. Yesterday, she only made two nasty remarks about you.

That's real progress."

"Honey, I'm not suggesting we stop. But an idea's been buzzing around my head."

"What is it this time?"

"You're going to think this one is even crazier than the last."

"Go on."

"Bernie," I looked at the floor. "What if it didn't have to be a pretence on my part? What if - if I could really learn to love her in whatever time she has left?"

"Honey! Wake up! This is the real world. You can't just turn on the love faucet on a Tuesday."

"I know. But I hate to be the kind of person who hates her mother. I want so much to love her."

"Just because you *want* to love someone doesn't mean -"

"I know. But, Bernie, I've been thinking and thinking about it. I can think of nothing else."

"I guess this means you're planning to go back to the drafting board. Back to Amos for more help," he sighed.

"Yes."

"You really want this very, very much, don't you, dear?"

* * * *

"Amos, I never imagined this would happen, but she's **really** responding. We've made a genuine dent in her. She still **makes** derogatory remarks about me, but fewer each time. She has softened up beyond recognition."

"Congratulations! You and Bernie really deserve an accolade."

"You expect me to be happy, Amos. But I'm not."

"Why not? Isn't this what you wanted?"

"No!"

"I don't understand."

"I don't want to go through a charade with her. Amos, now that she's softer and sweeter, I'm beginning to see what lay under all that armor all those years. Amos," my eyes filled. "Amos, I don't want to pretend to love her. I want the real thing. I want a real relationship."

Amos took a deep breath. His lips moved but he said nothing.

"Amos, I want to really love her in the time we have left."

"What does Bernie say?"

"He thinks it's totally unrealistic. That you can't turn a love faucet on. But, honestly, if you'd see how she responds to us. Like a thirsty flower to water. It's so touching. It's like she was hungry all her life for something that she couldn't name, and now we're giving it to her. Or maybe she's wanted to make up with me for years but didn't know how. Amos, I want a real relationship with her."

Amos stared at me. "I don't know what to say."

"I sure can't have it if I continue to stay detached."

"You want my permission to stop being detached."

"Yes. Why don't you say something?"

"I'm thinking."

"And?"

"I'm thinking that you're asking an awful lot of yourself."

"So?"

"The best answer I can give you is that you cannot drop your present behavior."

"I know. I know."

"Remember, we said that, hopefully, she would perceive the way you're treating her as 'love'? Well, it's, apparently, happened. She's responding to it. You're extremely fortunate."

"Yes, but -"

"You say you don't want to continue with the facade."

"I can't stand it."

"You don't have to continue with the facade. You have to continue to treat her as you've been doing. But not as a facade and not in order to manipulate her. But because you know it's what she needs and you want to give her what she needs so she'll be happier."

I sighed. "Amos, I'm willing to continue doing all that. But that alone won't -"

"That's only the beginning. To have a real relationship with her, you'll have to -"

"I know what you're going to say because I've come to that conclusion myself. To have a real relationship, I'd have to work on trying to understand how she became the kind of person she became, to get more of a handle on why she hated me so much. To get more - better - deeper insight into her own life."

"Exactly, Sylvia. If you can understand how she became the kind of person she became, you might develop compassion for her. And out of compassion, love may grow. Who knows?"

* * * *

"Where do we begin?" I asked the next day.

"We never really delved very much into why she built up such animosity to you," said Amos.

"Amos, I've spent decades trying to figure that one out. You might say I've been thinking of nothing else all my life."

"And?"

"Remember many years ago when I was in therapy, you asked me for my earliest memory which would have been in Istanbul, and I said I occasionally had a fleeting image of something that happened when I was about three, of being surrounded by legs, by women's bare legs."

"I remember very well."

"Well, the other day something shook me up so much I couldn't even share it with Bernie. His little granddaughter came to visit and sat on her potty in our bedroom near the window with the orange sunset reflected in Long Island Sound. And I had such an eerie feeling of deja vu, I can hardly bear to talk about it."

Amos looked entranced. "Go on."

"I must have told you the circumstances under which my parents married and went to Istanbul."

"Tell me again. It's been a long time."

"Well, my mother's family, the Koppels, were poised to emigrate to Palestine as soon as they could find a way out of the Soviet Union and she longed to join them there. But my father refused. He wanted to join his sister and mother in the U.S."

"Yes. I remember that."

"Istanbul was, therefore, a compromise for both my parents. They spent three whole years there, the three years of my infancy, fighting out this basic problem of their lives."

"That's right. I remember you told me your father had a good job with the Turkish Steamship Lines."

"Your memory is terrific. Yes, it was such a well-paying job that he was able to rent for us the most beautiful apartment in Istanbul - in Perra, the European quarter, on a hill overlooking the Bosphorus. Amos, you may think I'm going off on a tangent but I'll get to the point in a minute. Where was I?"

Amos smiled. "You were living in the most beautiful apartment in Istanbul."

"Yes. You see, my mother, coming from a huge, warm, close-knit family, was appalled by her loneliness. So my parents' first consideration was to find a lively neighborhood. Finally, they found the perfect apartment. It was enormous with murals on the walls and picture windows overlooking the colorful streetscape of mosques and minarets."

"You actually remember all that?"

"No. But my father who loved talking so much about Istanbul in his youth told me, and now it all came back to me.

"What my mother liked most about this apartment, however, was that it shared a balcony with an adjoining apartment where cheerful, well-dressed people always seemed to be coming and going."

"Sylvia, this is a long introduction to your story." He looked at his watch.

"I'm getting there. You'll soon see why the background is important. My mother both envied and took vicarious pleasure in the warm atmosphere of her neighbors' convivial family until, after some months, finally, she realized it was a whorehouse!"

Amos guffawed.

"In the meantime, I had integrated myself with my neighbors - young women who, unable to have children of their own, lavished lots of love on a baby! Amos, these were the barelegged women in the haunting memory where I am somehow sitting on the floor, and they are surrounding me! The barelegged women were the whorehouse women! They have to be!" I drew a deep breath. "I distinctly remember sitting on my potty on the spacious balcony on the hill facing the spectacular view of the Bosphorus with the sunset in all its glorious shades of orange spread out against the sky. When I finished, I brought my potty to my friends in the whorehouse to show everyone what I had accomplished. As always, I got a roar of laughter and a round of applause."

"Wonderful, Sylvia! And what is the clearest part of that memory?"

"The sunset and the applause."

"Can you attach a feeling to that part of your memory?"

"I was happy."

"Why?"

"I felt important. I had the attention of lots of people. I feel good when I think of that memory."

"How do you feel?"

"Like I have a piece of that orange sunset inside me. But that's not the end of my memory. There's a whole second part."

"Okay. Go on then."

"Just then, Mama stormed in. 'Oh, I'm so sorry,' she said. 'Is she making a pest of herself again? Her father spoils her so much she thinks the whole world revolves around her.'

"She shoved me out of the room so fast I felt she was sweeping me out with a broom. She glared at me, 'I told you not to bother them with your nonsense!'

"I said, 'But, Mama, the ladies _liked_ me!'

"And she muttered under her breath. 'Look at the way they fuss over her! You'd think no child ever sat on a potty before. No one ever made a fuss like that over me when I was a baby!'"

"And what's the clearest part of this second memory?"

"My mother screaming at me."

"Can you attach a feeling to that part of the memory?"

"How shattered I was. My beautiful bubble of happiness was blown to bits."

"You said the clearest part of the memory was her screaming."

"Yes."

"Let's focus in. What part of her screaming?"

"When she said my father spoils me so much I think the whole world revolves around me. That hurt."

"Let's concentrate on her. Why do you think she said that?"

"Envy."

"Sounds like it. And it ties in with what she said later."

"Yes. When she said so bitterly, 'No on ever fussed over me like that when I was a baby'. That's pure envy. Why should I have a better life than she had? What a ghastly thing to say to a child!"

There was a long pause.

"So," Amos puffed on his pipe. "what have we learned today?"

"This whole Istanbul memory. It gives me a lot of insight into why my mother treated me as she did."

"And that is?"

"Her envy that perhaps my father was showing me more love than her father had ever shown her. What else? I think her envy that I was having a better life than she had ever had."

"Excellent. Anything else?"

"Let's see. I don't know. Maybe - Yes! I have it! Her envy that I was getting loving attention for doing so little where she had done so much!"

"Great, Sylvia. Now there's one more aspect of all this we have to look at." He fixed his blue gaze on me. "How does all this make you feel about her?"

"Angry."

"Angry at whom?"

"Angry at my mother."

"Think carefully, Sylvia. Which mother are you angry at?"

"Oh," I thought a moment. "Oh, I see what you mean."

"Tell me."

"I think I do, that is."

"Go on."

"The little three year old Sylvia is angry at the thirty-three year old mother."

"Right. And, as I told you many years ago, the helpless little girl who needed love from her strong, powerful mother and got only inappropriate envy, had every right to be angry at her. But what about now?"

"What about now?"

"Yes. What about now?"

I stared at him. "I see what you mean. I'm not a child. I'm not helpless now."

"Go on, Sylvia."

"You're saying is there any point in me at my present age and in my prime in carrying this anger over to a totally different person? My eighty-four year old mother."

"What do you think?"

"There's no way she can hurt me now." I thought a moment. "She's old and helpless."

"Right."

"Now she's the one who's helpless."

"Yes."

"And probably completely unaware she's parroting old, old deeply ingrained patterns of behavior." I heaved a deep sigh. "And if I understand that, and I remain detached, she has no power to hurt me in any event. In fact," a new thought hit me, "our roles have reversed. I'm *her* mother now."

Chapter 15

It was our seventh visit in two weeks, and we were taking my mother out to lunch in Sheepshead Bay.

"I'll help you on with your overshoes," said Bernie.

My mother looked delighted to be getting so much attention from a gallant young man. After all, Bernie was only sixty-three.

As he picked up her foot to put it into her overshoe, Bernie, primed again by me, remarked, "Zvi, did you ever notice what small feet your mother has? They're so much smaller than yours."

"And all her life she's had a slim, lovely figure, too. She's never gained a pound."

My mother appeared to be absorbing our compliments through her pores. Her face had become smoother, less tense. The angry lines were melting away.

"That's right," she said. "I never allowed myself to get fat like some women."

We drove her to Sheepshead Bay.

"Now there are several restaurants here. And they all specialize in fish. In fact, there's a place where you can eat freshly caught fish, straight from the boat. They fry it right in front of you."

"Okay," said my mother as we helped her out of the car.

I exchanged glances with Bernie. Never in my life had I known her to be so agreeable.

We watched some men taking freshly caught fish from a large net and placing them on a table on horses on the sidewalk.

"Smell the fish, Ma?" I knew she didn't see well and thought smelling the fish would be interesting to her.

"I like the feel of the sun on my skin," said my mother, holding up her face to it.

It was the first positive statement, I had ever heard her make voluntarily in my entire life.

"That's right. You haven't been out in the sun for a long time. First Pa was sick for so long. Then, you began to have trouble with your eyes."

"I took care of Pa for many years."

"I know, Ma. You took good care of him."

We entered the restaurant.

"All my life I've taken care of others. Of all the seven sisters, I did the most for my family."

The waitress took our orders.

"Oh, I know that."

"How do you know? Did somebody say so?"

"Sure. Your sisters in Israel. Rivka. Layah. Malka. Ettie."

"They remember me?"

"Of course! They talked about you a lot. They love you very much."

Tears welled up in her eyes. "They remember me. They still remember me. After all these years."

"Of course. They told me many things about you."

"What did they say?"

"Oh, they said that when any of the younger children needed something, they knew they could come to you. You were a mother to all of them. And they told me how well you sang. How they used to call you 'the nightingale.'"

She broke into a smile, the first smile I had ever seen on her.

"Yes. That's what they used to call me."

"And they talked about how you used to have so many boy-friends."

She sighed. "Ach, the men I could have married! Did I ever tell you I could have married Agnon? But my father wouldn't let me. He said he wasn't good enough. That he'd never amount to anything. And do you know, Agnon later won the Nobel prize for Literature in Israel. I could have been Mrs. Agnon."

"It would have been nice to be a 'somebody'."

I had reflected her thought. A look of satisfaction crossed her face. It was as Amos had said. There's no greater gratification than to feel visible to someone.

"Ah, yes."

Our fish arrived, and we began to eat it.

"Is the fish good?" asked Bernie.

"Very good," said my mother.

Another positive statement. We were both stunned again.

"Did I ever tell you I could have married Chaim-Aaron?"

"I'm not sure. Tell me again. Anyway, Bernie hasn't heard it."

"I came from one of the most prestigious families in Russia, did you know that, Bernie?"

"I think Zvi mentioned it."

"My father came from a long line of *gaonim*. Talmudic geniuses. Going back to the sixteenth century. And our house in Odessa was always full of scholars." Her face lit up with nostalgia. "And they sat around in the evenings drinking tea from the samovar in tall red glasses. You know. Red from the tea. And talking and talking. Such important people used to visit us. Bialik and... Where was I?"

"You were beginning to say that you could have married Chaim-Aaron, Ma."

"Oh, yes. My father didn't have money for dowries for seven daughters. And, besides, he didn't believe in matchmakers."

"How did he expect his daughters to get married?" asked Bernie.

"My father always said the Koppel 'yichus' in itself was a dowry. You know what 'yichus' means, Bernie?"

"Prestige. Lineage. Something like that."

"Say, you really have a Jewish young man there!" exclaimed my mother.

"Yes," I smiled. "Bernie has all kinds of virtues. Go on, Ma."

"Oh, yes. Saturday afternoons all the men who were courting my father's daughters would come for tea. And my father and brothers would look them over."

"Not your mother?" I asked.

"No. My mother was busy with the inn. Besides, she was always pregnant. No. Saturday afternoon was for men."

"And evenings?"

"Evenings, too. Where was I? Oh, yes. When I was seventeen, Chaim-Aaron began to come on Saturdays. Oy, that Chaim-Aaron! How handsome he was! Such blue eyes! He came every single Saturday for six months. He and I looked into each other's eyes and looked into each other's eyes. But there was nothing - nothing at all we could do without my father's permission." Her voice drooped, and her face became overcast. "Finally, Chaim-Aaron asked my father who was his cousin, 'Would it be alright if I took Dvorahleh out for a walk?' My father said only one word, 'No!' That was it! There was nothing either of us could do." All the light drained out of her face. "I never saw Chaim-Aaron again. He married someone else. And," she sighed. "I still love him."

"Why did your father say, 'No!'?" asked Bernie.

She looked down at the table. "I don't know."

"Why didn't you ask him?" asked Bernie.

"I couldn't ask my father questions!"

"Aw, I'm sorry, Ma."

My mother was still lost in the past. "Chaim-Aaron also became a 'somebody'. He was one of the founders of the Technion in Haifa."

"And you married Pa who was a 'nobody'." I said.

She looked at me gratefully as if I had read her mind.

"I married the wrong man." She heaved a deep sigh. Then she met my eye meaningfully. "But I think you married the right one."

She had, finally, noticed how different my relationship with Bernie was from the one she had had with my father. As she spoke, I had the distinct feeling that it had been on the tip of her tongue to finish her sentence with "...although I can't see how you did it." But that she had bitten back the words. Instead, I read in her expression a tiny bit of grudging respect.

It felt good.

"Yes, Ma," I put my arms around Bernie. "I think I did."

Chapter 16

"This is the day we start talking about my mother's life," I said as I sat down in Amos' office that night.

He nodded.

"Bernie and I really had a great visit with her today. I'll tell you about that later. Now I want to get to the past. You know this delving is taking so much out of me. It's so hard to peel away the parent and see my mother not only as a parent who failed me, but as a human being in her own right."

"You feel that in the past your anger at the way she treated you prevented you from seeing her as a person."

"Sure. I came here for you to help me find the woman she is under her parent role."

"Not many people take the trouble to do that, Sylvia."

"I have to." I took a deep breath. "So - how do I start?"

"Pick a place."

"It's impossible to understand my mother at all unless you see her within the context of her family. Did I tell you anything about it?"

"Sylvia, it's been years. But it just happens I've been reading my old notes on you. Your mother's father was an overbearing patriarch. But his children revered him."

"That's right. He appeared to have all kinds of talents. He was erudite and wise and a great chess player. People came to consult him. And he certainly showed talent in producing children. But, of course, he had no way of making a living for them"

We both smiled.

"How did they live?"

"My grandmother kept an inn. But, since she was always pregnant, the entire burden of looking after the inn fell on the oldest daughter, my mother, Dvorah. My mother and I have talked so little over the years that I didn't know what I'm about to tell you till a few days ago. But just the other day, she confided in Bernie and me.

From the time she was seven, once a week, she had been given a huge pile of linen to wash. She would pile it onto a cart and drag it down to the river in Berdichev where they lived at the time. There, she would pound the laundry on the rocks till it was clean."

"How does that story make you feel?"

"For three days, I haven't been able to get it out of my mind. Just think of that poor little seven year old pounding the wash on the rocks even in winter when she had to break the ice to get to the freezing water. Today, we'd call her an abused or at least an exploited child. But I know she showed no outward resentment to either of her parents. She certainly never talked back to them. She held her father in awe."

"What do you think happened to her resentment?"

"She buried it, I suppose."

"Remember we once discussed the fact that the emotions we bury are those which control our lives? Here's a perfect example. What happens to buried resentment that's not directed at the person we resent?"

I sighed. "It comes out in other subterranean ways."

"Like?"

"My mother spread hers around for the rest of her life. To everyone! But, she, especially, passed it on to me."

"Yes. Unless such a person siphons his resentment off through therapy he nearly always passes it on to the next generation."

"Something to think about, Amos, isn't it?"

"She never got a brother to help her with the wash? Or were they too young?"

"No. In fact, one, Dovid, was three years older than she. But that particular brother was considered a genius. They wouldn't make him waste his time on something as menial as the wash. He was studying at some fancy Yeshiva. Although from what my mother has told me, I gather all the boys in the family lived in a totally different world from the girls."

"A caste system."

"Exactly. The upper caste consisted of the men - the lower

caste, the women whose sole purpose in life was to serve them. As a matter of fact, that's how my mother expected me to live - to go to work at fourteen so my brother would be assured of enough funds for college. That's precisely what happened in her family. All the seven sisters went to work at early ages, my mother was a kindergarten teacher, and brought their pay to their father untouched. The money was not for them! They could not save it for dowries. The money was for their brothers' education."

"How do you feel about all that?"

"How do I feel! I'm appalled at the injustice of it. But what gets me is that my mother was not appalled. Quite the contrary. She carried all this over into the next generation. Into what she expected of me. She never questioned anything about her family. Her father's decisions were the decisions of God."

"Now you're getting a good handle on her value system. But the fact that she accepted everything is in itself part of her value system. You don't question God. Can you remember when you were in therapy last time. How you told me you had accepted everything your mother told you about yourself - hook, line, and sinker?"

"I know."

"Okay. Back to your mother. What was the tone of that memory your mother reported of washing the linen down by the river?"

"Tone?"

"What were her feelings about it?"

"Let's see. What was it she said? Oh, that she had been the best, the most sacrificing of all seven daughters. That she had done the most for her family. No. Wait. She said more. She said that while she was pounding the clothes in the river, she was foolish enough to think that maybe God was watching and would make it all up to her some day by giving her a wonderful husband and daughter who was as good to her as she had been to her parents."

"So maybe she did have a glimmer that she was being exploited."

"That's right. If she wanted compensation, it meant there was something to compensate for. She just never dared bring the feeling up to her consciousness." I paused and took a deep breath. "Amos, this is fascinating! Imagine! This seven year old actually had a secret pact with God! A hidden agenda."

"That *is* fascinating!"

"Yes. And I really think she lived by that agenda all her life. She certainly never changed it. Or brought it up to date."

"Right." He puffed at his pipe. "Let's look at this hidden agenda from another angle, Sylvia. What do you think it may have done to her relationship with men?"

I thought for a moment. "It seems to me that if you're seeking a husband who will make up to you for past injustices of such magnitude, you're doomed."

"Go on."

"You're doomed to failure. I mean, what man could ever live up to that and compensate you enough?"

"What man indeed? Did your father?"

"What are you talking about? My father was an especially horrendous choice for her to have made."

I stopped myself.

"Go on, Sylvia. He was an especially horrendous choice for her to have made."

"Because he had a hidden agenda of his own."

"Tell me about your father's hidden agenda," said Amos the next day.

"Well, briefly, when my father was only twelve, he lost his father, who was not only wealthy, but, according to him, the best human being who had ever lived. And for the rest of his life, he saw himself as a 'poor helpless orphan,' thrown to the wolves. That feeling of being an orphan stayed with him. When he was seventy-two, he was still talking of himself as a poor orphan.

"And his hidden agenda was that God surely owed him something to compensate for this enormous loss he had sustained which had robbed him of all the opportunities this wonderful father might have provided for him. Surely he would make it up to him by giving him a wife who would cater to his every whim. Wasn't it the least he deserved?"

We both smiled.

"Very interesting. So each of your parents sought compensation from the other for damages sustained, for past inequities."

"Quite a match! You can see why it was the kind of marriage it was!"

"But your mother also sought compensation from you."

"Yes. The day I was born, I was handed a bill for what I owed her. After that, there was nothing I could ever do that was right. Or good enough. Amos, this is really blowing my mind. I could never understand why nothing I ever did pleased her. But, seen from her viewpoint, it's starting to make sense. All this disparagement of me for all those years, all those decades." Tears sprang to my eyes. "I'm beginning to see it had nothing to do with me." My voice broke. "It had to do with her own needs. She never saw me at all. She wore blinders." I sat sobbing. I needed time to absorb this insight that had come to me only as I voiced it.

There was a long silence.

"Exactly, Sylvia," said Amos softly.

I took a deep, ragged breath, blinking away my tears.

"Amos, I hope these 'insights' don't interfere with my current relationship with her. I have to remember to keep what I'm feeling directed at the young mother. Not at my mother as she is today."

"You will, I'm sure," Amos looked at me approvingly. "One more thing. About your brother. She never sought compensation from him?"

"Mitch? Oh, she sanctified him as one of the male geniuses of her family, the Koppel family. Nothing he could ever do was wrong. All that was expected of him was that he be as brilliant as her brothers so she could be proud of him."

"Poor Mitch," smiled Amos.

"She even called him by her brother's name when she got excited. Since I could do no right and he could do no wrong, you can imagine the kind of relationship we had. It was ghastly."

"What happened to Mitch?"

"He found his halo so tight that he ran off to California nearly eighteen years ago and never came back. He's a publicist or something. Gets divorced a lot."

We both smiled.

"Amos, I want to tie up a few more ends about my mother's life. About her father, especially. I think they're very important."

I told him how her father refused to give her the singing lessons she longed for. How he would not allow her to marry Agnon because "he never would amount to anything." Most of all, how he had put a sharp end to her romance with Chaim-Aaron whom she adored and, indeed, loved to this day.

"I wonder how much of her repressed anger at her father came out against her husband?" asked Amos.

"I wonder," I said thoughtfully. "But Amos, her husband, my father, was almost exactly like her father. He also frustrated her at every turn. Remember I once told you how she was supposed to give that concert at the Pioneer Women, something she had eagerly been looking forward to for months, and he didn't come home to be with the children that night, and she couldn't go. She wanted to kill him that night. I don't think she ever really forgave him.

"And all her life, she was dying to live in Israel where she could be with her family to whom she was so attached. And he not only refused to live there, he even refused to visit. She was blazing with anger at him all her life. You might say with good reason."

Amos was silent for a long time. "I wonder how much of this anger at your father she foisted onto you?"

That insight was so overwhelming that I walked into a door on my way out.

Chapter 17

My mother looked delighted to see us the following morning.

"I enjoy your visits not only because I enjoy your company, but because it shows me how much Bernie must love you if he's willing to come so often."

I was dumbfounded. "Bernie is a very loving husband, but he's also a very decent person. Since I don't drive highways, it would be very hard for me to get here without him." I smiled at him.

I could not tell how much my mother could see. But she appeared to be staring at us. Or rather staring in our direction. Her mouth opened, then shut, then opened again. She seemed to be struggling to formulate a thought. Finally, she found the words. "I see you understand life." By that, I understood her to mean that I knew how to treat my husband in such a way that he would want to be good to me. I knew it was the highest accolade she could have paid me.

Totally nonplussed, I was still thinking of a response when she said softly under her breath. "Sometimes the eggs are wiser than the chickens."

My mother had agreed to see an eye doctor, and we drove her for her appointment that morning.

He immediately sent us to a glaucoma specialist who told us we had waited too long. He would operate as soon as possible. Her heart was strong. The operation posed no danger, but he held out little hope.

On the way home from the specialist, I expected my mother to be dejected. It turned out her mind was on something else entirely. When I stepped into a pharmacy for a moment to get her some medication she turned to Bernie and said, "I'm so happy! Here I thought I would die with Zviah hating me!"

Bernie, of course, reported this to me immediately, to my great joy.

This gave me the courage, later in the day, to say to her, "Ma, you see how well you and I can get along? Now why were you so mean to me all those years?"

She made no answer but just stood there looking absolutely stricken with guilt. Big tears trickled down her cheeks and fell onto her blouse.

But I didn't really need her answer.

"It was because you were so angry at Pa all your life yet you couldn't show him all your anger because you needed him too much. So you took it out on me because I was his favorite child."

Very slowly she nodded, her tears coming faster, her face working.

I went over to her and put my arms around her, and we hugged for the very first time in our lives!

It was the most gratifying thing that ever happened to me.

I could feel my mother, so tiny and thin and fragile, trembling in my arms.

Part 6

Peace

Chapter 18

My mother had her operation. Unfortunately, it was not successful. While she would be able to perceive light and some shadowy objects, she would have no real vision.

The day after the operation when I went to see her, she was confused from the anesthetic. She still wore bandages on her eyes but beamed when she heard my voice. "Zviah, you'll never guess what happened! Chaim-Aaron came to see me last night! He brought me flowers!"

She had not seen Chaim-Aaron for nearly seventy years!

"That's lovely, Ma. I'm so glad he still remembers you."

"He still loves me."

At this point, I hated to take her back to her apartment, only to have to remove her at some later point to go to the Home for the Blind. I had an even greater problem. I had spent weeks building this relationship with her which was so important to both of us. If I now suggested she go to the Home for the Jewish Blind, wasn't there a strong danger that she would suspect that all the love I had shown her had been false for the purpose of winning her confidence so she would agree to go?

I was truly in a quandary. I decided that she must be encouraged to go to the Home. But that the suggestion should come not from me but from the hospital Social Worker. I had a talk with the Social Worker and found her most receptive. She promised to speak to my mother as soon as she felt her mind was clear enough to absorb what she was saying.

I kept seeing my mother every day but did not broach the subject. After about four days, my mother herself brought it up.

"Zviah, I have to talk to you about something. The Social Worker here, Frieda, has been telling me that it would be better for me to go to the Home for Jewish Blind. They have Jewish programs, and I'd be able to sing at them."

I had, of course, primed Frieda as to what to say to my

mother. When I had visited the Home, I had learned from the Social Worker there that they did indeed welcome people with my mother's talents and would encourage them.

I was so delighted, I could hardly speak. "Oh, yes, they do have such programs. They have a very good musical department."

"Maybe it would be better for me to be there than to be all alone at home."

"Oh, much, much better, Ma." How had this miracle happened? My mother was thinking as a logical person.

"I even thought of living with you."

Oh, not that, I prayed. I was getting along so well with my mother now, but I would not wish to test the relationship by living together. She was very likely to have setbacks that might undo everything I had worked so hard for. I clenched my fists.

"But since I can't see, it would be hard to live in a new house where I don't know my way around. And you wouldn't be able to leave me alone."

"And our house has stairs in unexpected places." It was an old Victorian house in Sea Cliff, and it really did.

My mother took my hand and began to speak confidentially. "I don't really want to go at all."

I prayed she wouldn't change her mind.

"After all, a Home is not a home." She smiled at her own joke.

My mother who had never made a joke in her life was developing a sense of humor. A sense of humor was a sure sign of sanity!

"But," she was still speaking thoughtfully. "I guess it's best. I don't want to be a burden on you and Bernie. I don't want you to have to come every day. After all, it's not as if I have seven daughters like my mother so one can come each day." I was flabbergasted at her new sensitivity.

"I think it's an excellent idea, Ma," I said. "I think it's very good for you to be with people, and they told me they have an excellent musical program and you'll be able to sing. We'll see you often."

"That's what Frieda said," said my mother. "So maybe you should make an application for me." She now trusted people!

She didn't know we had made the application more than a month ago!

* * * *

Our next project was to have my mother interviewed by a psychiatrist to ascertain that she was well-adjusted. Despite my mother's recent and current sanity, I was terrified at what a psychiatrist might uncover under close scrutiny. I knew I had to pick the psychiatrist very, very carefully. That very day I began to investigate the psychiatrists on the list given me by the Jewish Home for the Blind. I got bios of seven and found something wrong with each one. Then I found the right one. He was an older man, in his sixties, which was good. I gathered from talking to people at the King's County Mental Health Association that he was a low key person. But, most important of all, he was an Israeli. Precisely, what I had been hoping to find.

The next day, the day she was discharged from the hospital, I brought my mother a suit of my own that was too tight for me. She swam in it but with jewelry looked rather elegant.

Naturally, I did not tell her that she was going to be interviewed by a psychiatrist, but merely that we were going to visit someone from Israel who happened to be a doctor.

The psychiatrist put her at ease, then asked her to tell him about herself. I reminded her that he was an Israeli, and she could speak Hebrew to him.

She immediately relaxed and opened the floodgates. She told him in Hebrew how her husband had brought her to America against her will, described the kind of family she came from, why she was so sorry to lose them, and went on to enumerate proudly the accomplishments of all her brothers starting with Dovid, the famous writer and translator, Hershel who had been Director of the Hadassah Hospital but had died young, etc. I don't think my mother had enjoyed an afternoon so much in decades. She got so carried away that after a while she said, "Doctor, maybe you'd like some more tea?"

He thanked her and reminded her that she had visited him! .

In the end, she made such a good impression on the doctor that he wrote a glowing recommendation about what a positive, well-adjusted person she was. He stated that he felt she had a great contribution to make to the Home for the Jewish Blind. I had explained how difficult it would be to have her leave the Hospital to return to her apartment and then later have to make yet another adjustment to the Home. I asked if he could ask them to accept her straight from the Hospital.

On the strength of his recommendation, the Home accepted her less than three weeks later. I had feared the worst, but she was able to spend those two and a half weeks with an aide without too much trouble.

* * * *

My mother became the star of the Jewish Guild Home for the Blind.

She had only one setback.

After placing her there, Bernie and I left immediately on a much needed vacation for a few days. When we returned, we found my mother hysterical. We had abandoned her! We had left her all alone among strangers! She had refused to eat and now weighed only eighty-two pounds.

I sent Bernie home and spent the next twenty-four hours with her, sleeping over at a motel, and comforting her.

After that, it was all roses. I had told the Social Worker at the Home that my mother was very adept at conducting Passover Seders and knew many melodies for every song in the Haggadah. Partly to placate her, I imagine, they allowed her to do so, and she acquitted herself splendidly. When I came to visit a few days later, her face was wreathed in smiles as she told me about it. "Now, I can use what I know," she told me happily.

She was the star of the Home for another reason as well.

Most of the old women there felt very bitter about their children who rarely came to visit. My mother never stopped talking about her loving daughter and son-in-law who visited every second week. The other women openly envied her, which she loved, and constantly commented on what a wonderful mother she must have been to have inspired such love not only in her daughter but even in her son-in-law. "What's your secret?" they all asked.

My mother glowed.

One day during the summer, Bernie found someone to talk to, and I took my mother out for a walk alone through the grounds of the Home. I made some remark about its beautiful setting on a low hill fringed by woods. "I'm so sorry you can't see it, Ma."

"I'm not sad I'm blind, Zviah. I'm happy I have you."

"That's a beautiful thing to say, Ma."

"I was just thinking," she had a dreamy look on her face. "I was thinking about Istanbul. You were such a beautiful baby."

Now she thought of me as a beautiful baby!

"I can remember one day when I dressed you up to go to the covered market they called the Souk. My neighbor said, 'With such a child you're going to the Souk?' There had been cases of children being stolen."

"That's an interesting memory. I wish I remembered more about Istanbul."

"Do you remember the carriage rides we used to take on Friday, the Turkish Sunday?"

"Not really. I was too young."

"You might remember. You were about three. We used to go for drives with Pa's colleague, a Turk who always wore a fez although it was forbidden."

"Why was it forbidden, Ma?"

"I'm not sure. Pa would know. I think it's because Ataturk wanted to make Turkey modern, so he banned the men from wearing fezes and the women from wearing veils. All the women wore veils anyway. I never saw a Turkish woman's face all the time I was there. What was I talking about?"

"About the carriage rides we used to take with Pa's colleague, the Turk."

"Oh, yes. We used to go driving every Friday. He came with his three wives, seated according to rank."

We both smiled.

"Pa and I and you used to sit across from them."

"Sounds very nice."

"And I remember one Friday in particular."

Her voice drifted away at this point.

"What did you say, Ma?"

"What was I talking about?"

"You were saying, you remembered one particular Friday."

"I can't remember what I wanted to say."

"Okay, Ma. Maybe it will come back to you."

We kept walking.

Then, she said, "Now I remember. One Friday, we were sitting on the two benches facing each other. You were on Pa's lap. And somehow you realized something was wrong. Because all the other children were cuddled on their mother's laps. But you were on your father's."

"You can remember all that, Ma?"

"Suddenly, it's so clear to me. As though it happened yesterday."

"Go on, Ma."

"I can remember the expression on your face. You were puzzled. And you looked from him to me. No. You gazed longingly at me." Her voice caught.

"Then you jumped off Pa's lap and tried to climb up on mine." She paused and collected her thoughts. "But I was wearing a new dress. I can still see it. It was ivory silk and had a pattern of little red birds flying on it."

"I think I remember that pattern. Didn't you later make a blouse out of it in Montreal?"

"Yes. It was a wonderful material. It never wore out. I loved that dress. I thought it set off my dark hair and ivory skin."

She stopped to catch her breath. Suddenly, her voice crumbled, and she sounded close to tears. "And because I was so proud of my dress I wouldn't let you get on my lap. I -" she swallowed. "I brushed you off. I said, 'Get off me. You'll crease my new dress. And your hands are sticky. Abraham, take her away from me!' I can still remember the look on your face, Zviah." She took my hand. "I was so foolish. The dress was more important to me than you were." Tears slid out of the corners of her eyes. "Zviah," her face was close to mine, "I'm so sorry."

My throat also felt clogged. Then I found my voice. "It's okay, Ma. It all worked out in the end."

"No. No, it didn't. I've caused - so much - so much..."

She seemed very tired at that point, and we returned to the Home.

* * * *

Another time Bernie and I visited, my mother whispered excitedly, "I've something very important to tell you."

We led her into the dining room so we could have privacy.

"Listen, Zviah, it's wonderful! I have a new suitor!"

I could hear Bernie stifling his laugh.

"He's just the kind of man I've always dreamed of. He has spent time in Israel. He knows Israel very well. He used to live on a kibbutz. He speaks Hebrew fluently. We talk in Hebrew all the time!" Her face shone. "And he knows all the same songs that I know. He wants me to give a concert for Chanuka. We've already picked out the songs. When I sing, he accompanies me on the piano. Zviah, he pays me so many compliments." She broke into an even more radiant smile. "You wouldn't believe it. I just know he loves me! I can feel it. There are four or five other women in the room but I heard him say, 'Dvorah is my best girl!'"

At that moment, I realized she was talking about the Recreation Director who ran the music programs and might have been singling her out because of her voice. Mark was a tall, red-headed man of about thirty-two who had a wife and two children.

"His name is Mark and he's very strong. I can feel his arm when he leads me out of the room. He told me how much he likes me so many times. That mine is the best voice he's heard in the Home in all the years he's been here." She ran out of breath. "I told him, 'Mark,' I said, 'You're too young for me.'"

Bernie couldn't suppress his laugh any longer and hurriedly left the room.

At that moment, Mark strode by. He must have gathered from the excited way my mother was speaking that she was talking about him for he flashed me a broad smile and winked.

"I wouldn't be surprised if Mark tries to speak to my father about me one of these days."

I was enjoying my mother!

"But, Zviah, I'm worried," she grabbed my wrist. "I'm afraid he has another woman. I know he's tall because his voice comes from high up. But sometimes he seems to have with him a woman who's short. Her voice comes from where I am. I don't want to lose him."

"I don't think you'll lose Mark, Ma. I think he values you too much."

* * * *

We had become friends. She was sharing with me what was important to her, as one girlfriend does with another!

* * * *

On another day, I said, "Ma, you always talk about your father. Never about your mother."

She thought for a moment. "How can you compare them? My mother had no education. She was married before she was fourteen."

On the next visit, however, she did begin to speak of her mother.

"Did I ever tell you that I had problems with my eyes even as a child? Bernie, did I ever tell you?"

"No."

"Yes. I was cross-eyed. But my mother knew just what to do. You must remember that in those days you didn't need fancy operations to solve problems. When I was five, my mother took me to Chaya de Kluge, Chaya the Wise One, who always had remedies for things like that. Chaya told my mother that she must take me into a very young pine forest exactly at dawn and walk with me for twenty minutes. But it had to be a very young forest, she cautioned us."

My mother sighed with satisfaction.

"The very next day, my mother got up at four o'clock. It was June, I remember. Then, she woke me up. She was very pregnant at that time and, in fact, gave birth in less than a month. But she took me to this young pine forest just outside of Berdichev." My mother inhaled deeply. "Ah, I can still remember how it smelled! Nothing in America smells like that! We walked and walked. Then we went home. And do you know, Bernie, would you believe this? My eyes straightened out! I had such beautiful eyes when I was a young girl!"

"Fantastic!" said Bernie.

"My mother really loved me. She once told me that someone had asked her how she could possibly love ten children equally and she replied, 'But I don't have ten children. I have one Dovid, and one Hershel and one Dvorah, and one Rivka... I love them all the same way. They are like the fingers of my two hands.'"

Neither my mother nor her mother ever realized how differently she and her husband treated their sons and daughters. They were treating the sons as sons were traditionally treated. They were treating daughters as *they* were traditionally treated. This did not mean they loved them any the less!

With the help of Mark's accompaniment and encouragement, my mother did give a Chanuka concert. It was a roaring success. It was so successful, in fact, that they asked her to give another one in February as a fund raiser for the Home. She did even better at that one. My mother was suffused with happiness. All her dreams had come true.

In the spring, after she had conducted the Passover Seder a second time, she and I went for another walk through the grounds.

It was a balmy day, but breezy.

"It's the kind of day you have on a ship," my mother, suddenly, said.

I knew she had had only one journey on a ship.

"You're thinking of the boat trip you took from Istanbul to Canada?" I asked.

"Yes!" she grabbed my hand. "How did you know?"

"It just occurred to me. But that trip was in the fall."

"That's right. It was October. But the weather was just like this."

I waited for my mother to say more. I knew it had been a terrible trip for her and was now so sorry I had mentioned it. I didn't know if she'd want to remember it.

"I was so miserable on that trip."

"I know, Ma. You don't have to talk about it. Let's talk about something else."

"No. I want to talk about it. I remember I lay in my room seasick - without eating. I hated to leave my family behind, and I was so afraid of going to Canada. I knew nothing about Canada."

"I know, Ma. It must have been very frightening to go to a place where you knew no one and didn't know the language."

She turned to me with gratitude. "And I remember how you came in to cheer me up, and you said that maybe I'd eat if you got me something I really like so you and Pa had gotten me some herring and olives from the waiter — and the herring and the big shiny black olives were on a beautiful plate with rosebuds all around the rim. I'll never forget that plate." Her voice broke.

Something jogged my memory. I felt goose bumps rise all over me! "Ma, I remember that plate, too."

"You do? Is it possible?"

"Honestly! The plate wasn't round. It was oval!"

We were better than girlfriends. We were girlfriends with

common memories going back fifty years!

"And I remember how I pushed the plate with the olives and herring to the floor - and how disappointed you were. Zviah! I can still see your face." She burst into sobs. "Zviah, what a fool I was. We're only given one life. Oh, God, if I only had it to do over again."

Chapter 19

We now had a routine. Each time Bernie and I came, she would say, "Oy, if you only knew what it means to me to have you come to visit me. What it means to me to have you kiss me!" Or "When you two come to see me, I feel so good!"

The following summer, she and I had another opportunity to go for a walk alone.

She told me again how much it meant to her to have made up with me. "I was so afraid I'd die with you hating me."

"You see, Ma. You're really so sweet underneath. Why were you so bitter all those years?"

She half smiled, steeped in her memories. "Sometimes, things happen that make you angry." She remained silent for a long time. I didn't want to intrude on her thoughts.

Finally, she said, "I was just thinking about Pa."

I was surprised. She had rarely mentioned him lately.

She sighed. "I was so angry at him for so many years. Boy! Did I give it to him! I never said a good word to him!" She stopped and took a deep breath. "If I could, I'd apologize to him!"

"You would?" I was stunned.

She heaved a deep sigh. "Maybe over there, where I'll soon be going, I'll meet him and apologize to him. I hope so." She fell silent.

I waited for her to say more. We kept walking.

Finally, she turned to me. "You see," she said, her eyes brimming, "I know why he refused to go to Palestine with me."

"You do?" I was astounded.

"Yes." She looked down for a moment, then up again at me. "It's because of that chess game."

"Chess game?" Now I remembered. She had once mentioned a chess game to Bernie and me on one of our early visits. Her exact words were that, since the chess game, she knew she had married the wrong man. I was puzzled about the connection of the chess game to Israel.

"Tell me about the chess game, Ma. Where did it take place?"

She sighed. "When Pa and I came back to Odessa from Volochisk to have the baby - you."

Suddenly, I was fascinated. That was precisely the time I was most curious about. What had happened around that time that completely shattered their relationship.

"Oh, yes. You came back with Pa and stayed with your parents."

"On Bazarnya Street, yes. Only some of my brothers and sisters were there then. Rivka and her husband, and - and..." She had trouble remembering their names, perhaps. "...and Malka and Layah." So she did remember. Her eyes wore a far away look. "And, of course, Dovid and Hershel."

"Yes, Ma. You were saying that you came back to have the baby, me, with your family."

"And my father decided he wanted to get to know his new son-in-law Abraham better."

I spotted a bench. "Ma, you want to sit down here?"

We sat down. My mother turned to me. "After all, my father had done something extraordinary when he let me marry Pa. He didn't really know him at all. And now he had been given a chance to get to know him." She gazed into the distance as though staring through time. "And, well, he looked him over - in his own way."

"What do you mean, his own way?"

"He challenged him to a game of chess. He always did that."

"A game of chess?" I couldn't believe what I was hearing.

"I can hear my father's voice so clearly. 'You do play, don't you, Abraham?' he asked. My heart sank. If Pa said, 'No,' the decision might go against him. But if he said, 'Yes,' and didn't prove to be a worthy opponent -." She sighed. "After all, my father was a master chess player in Odessa, a city of master chess players."

"What happened then?" I was getting excited.

"Abraham said 'yes'. I closed my eyes and prayed. My hands were clenched so hard my nails were making holes in my palms."

She closed her eyes and clenched her fists.

She stayed that way so long I thought she had fallen asleep.

"Ma! Ma!" I touched her arm.

She opened her eyes. "Oh, you're still here?"

"Ma, you fell asleep?"

"Did I? I don't know. Maybe."

I waited.

"I was reliving."

"Yes, Ma. You were reliving?"

"The chess game! They began to play, my father and Abraham. The entire family kept their eyes on them. They followed each move. Abraham kept creasing his brow, running his fingers through his hair, inside his collar. He was pondering each move. My father moved with ease and speed. He conquered Abraham's knights one by one. He captured his bishop. He was poised to take his queen!"

My mother was breathing hard.

"Yes, Ma. And what happened then?"

Her face fell. "Abraham made a bad move. My father pounced and demolished him."

"Yes, Ma. And then?"

She looked down at the ground. "Everyone knew that Abraham didn't stand a chance now. Moreover, without anyone saying a word, Abraham knew it." She closed her eyes again. I felt she was seeing a scene indelibly etched in her mind. "And he could see - in their eyes - I mean, he could..."

"He could see the pity in their eyes."

"Yes. That's it!"

"Go on, Ma."

She stopped. She seemed to be looking deep inside herself.

"But it was more than just pity. He sensed the family's...There's something more I wanted to say."

"Go on, Ma."

"That they - Why can't I find the words? That they..."

"That they condemned him as a loser?"

"Oh yes! Yes! But more."

"Go on."

"Oh, it's so hard. So hard to think. It gives me such a headache."

"You're doing fine, Ma."

"No."

"What did Pa do then?"

"He turned red as a beet. He picked up his coat. He didn't look left or right. He just slunk out of the room and the house."

She sat there, her face flushed. She looked defeated.

"And then? What did you do?"

"Nothing. That's the whole point. I just sat there."

"You didn't go after him?"

"I couldn't move." She looked guilty. "I told my sister, Rivka, that I never - I never should have married him," she sounded hoarse.

"But why, Ma?"

Her face was working. Tears ran down her cheeks. "I was stupid. I felt he had committed - an - something for which I could never forgive him."

"What?"

"He had disgraced me. Well, he had disgraced himself, first of all. But in the process, he had disgraced me."

"How had he disgraced you?"

"Look, if he knew my father was a master chess player, how did he have the chutzpah to accept the challenge?"

I was too stunned to speak.

"And it seemed to me that now I knew Abraham simply didn't measure up to the Koppels."

"Ma!"

"And that everyone else in the family knew it. They never respected him after that. You should see the way Dovid and Hershel and even my sisters..."

"But you just said you had been stupid. That meant that later you realized something else."

"Oh, yes. Just lately, since I've grown blind, I see so much. Now I see how stupid I was. Abraham always felt that my first loyalty should have been to him. And that my father shouldn't have challenged him if he knew he was a much better player. But how could I see it at the time? I always thought my father was..."

"I'm sure Pa, also, felt that, even if your father did challenge him, you might have said something like 'Papa, Abraham is a wonderful man and I love him, but he's no chess player. Please don't embarrass him.' That you might at least have forewarned him."

She sat nodding.

"Oy, Zviah, if I only had my life to live over again, I'd treat him differently. I wish I could apologize to him. Naturally, he didn't want to go to Israel where he'd meet this family who would snub him again, who would make him feel small."

She rocked back and forth, hugging her knees.

"A whole lifetime. A whole wasted lifetime."

Then she took my arm. "Come let's go back. It's getting cold."

As we walked, she said. "But, maybe my life wasn't wasted. If I hadn't married Pa, I wouldn't have had you."

*   *   *   *

After that she began to decline. She was moved from the Health Related Facilities Section of the Home to the Nursing Home section, a very unpleasant place to visit. Her mind was still much clearer than most of the people there who were suffering from Alzheimer's, but she was getting harder to communicate with and could no longer walk.

When we returned from a three week trip to Europe, we found she had had a stroke.

The day we visited, I was appalled at the way she looked. Her face seemed broken in two. One half was stiff and rigid. The other half wobbled. She couldn't speak, but, when she heard my voice, she burst into sobs. She tried to form words and, when they wouldn't come out as words, grew more and more frustrated and began to cry and scream.

I stroked her head.

"Ma, I know it's been awful for you. You got sick and had no one to turn to. And you couldn't even talk to tell anyone how you felt. It must be awful not to be able to talk."

I could see she had registered what I said because she stopped screaming.

I took her in my arms and held her.

Gradually, she relaxed, snuggled into my arms and fell asleep.

She died the following day without waking up. She was either ninety or ninety-one. I had never known her exact age.

When, after her death, I thanked Mark for all the help he had given her, he smiled, "Our greatest success story!"

The End